DEFINITELY FOREVER

BOOK THREE IN DEFINITELY SERIES

ELLA MILES

FREE BOOKS

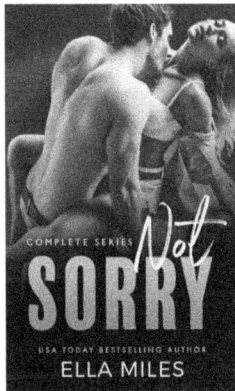

Read **Not Sorry** for **FREE**! And sign up to get my latest
releases, updates, and more goodies
here→EllaMiles.com/freebooks

Follow me on BookBub to get notified of my new releases
and recommendations here→Follow on BookBub Here

Join Ella's Bellas FB group for giveaways and a **FREE** copy of **Pretend I'm Yours**→Join Ella's Bellas Here

MAYBE, DEFINITELY SERIES

MAYBE, DEFINITELY SERIES:

Maybe Yes
Maybe Never
Maybe Always

Definitely Yes
Definitely No
Definitely Forever

1

BEAST

"Is it mine?" I ask.

"No."

That word kills me, destroys me. It was absolutely the last thing I expected when I came here today. I expected Scarlett would be upset with me. I expected she would yell. I expected she would kick me out.

But I also expected I could eventually convince her that I loved her. I thought I could convince her that I'd changed, that I could continue to change for her. I thought I could convince her to let me protect her with some work on my part.

But that one little word has changed all those thoughts. That one little word has destroyed any chance of any of that ever happening. That one little word has destroyed me.

I've been frozen since that word fell from her lips. I could hear the anger in her voice as she said that word. She had known what that word would do to me. But I also felt the tiniest bit of sadness. On some level, that means she still cares about me.

I take a deep breath for the first time in minutes after

she told me my world was over. I close my eyes as I breathe. I can already feel the pain sinking into my chest. I can already feel it spreading throughout my body.

I take another deep breath and open my eyes. I look across the darkness at Beauty, who is standing frozen as well, staring at me. I don't know what is going through her mind right now. I don't know what she is thinking. But I can feel her pain with every breath. And I have to know why she is putting herself through so much pain. *For whom?*

"Whose is it?"

"We aren't doing this, Beast."

I wince when she says the word *Beast*. It no longer feels like an endearment. It feels like a knife being shoved into my heart.

I watch her turn to walk away from me, heading toward the door to get me to leave, but I can't leave yet. Not without answers. I have to know why she's destroyed everything that could have been.

I run toward her and step between her and the door. "Stop."

She does.

"Whose baby is it? You owe me that, don't you think?"

She shakes her head. "I don't owe you anything. You lied to me. You tested me. You hurt me. I moved on. That's all you need to know."

She tries to push by me, but I grab her arm, quickly stopping her in her tracks.

"Please."

I can hear her swallow as she contemplates my request. It's pathetic—my begging, my *pleading*. I'm not used to such words falling from my lips. I'm used to hearing that word falling from her lips when my cock is buried deep inside her.

She takes a deep breath, and I watch her chest rise and fall. I know she's in pain, just like I am.

She shakes her head, but doesn't say a word. She doesn't answer me.

I run a hand through my hair, trying not to let the defeat overwhelm me, like it so easily could. If I let it, I'll do something crazy, like go out and kill whomever I think the father is. I can't do that. I have to think straight. At least, I can't kill someone until I'm sure who the motherfucker is.

"I need to know who destroyed us, Scarlett. I need to know who took away the only good thing in my life, Scar," I say. I don't know why I called her Scar. I never have before, but it feels like I'm pleading with a best friend instead of a lover. Instead of the woman I want to spend all my life with. If I don't have her, I'm not sure what's the point of continuing my life.

To protect her.

"You're the reason we aren't together. You're the reason we can never be together. Don't blame the guy who knocked me up. Long before he came around, you made it clear we could never be together."

She brushes past me this time, and I watch in horror as she walks to the door. There is nothing left to do short of throwing her over my shoulder, tying her up, and torturing her until she tells me who did this to her. But her words ring in my ear. It was me. This is my fault. I did this. I'm the monster here, not anyone else.

I just need to get out of her life before I destroy anything else. Before I cause her any more pain.

I walk toward the door that Scarlett has her hand on, ready to throw me out the second she can't handle talking to me anymore, which I know is only seconds away from happening. I know she is seconds away from tears staining her cheeks, and I know she won't let me see her cry. Not today. Not after what I did to her.

I stop a foot away from her, but it doesn't stop me from asking again because I have to know. I have to know that she and the baby are going to be taken care of. I need to know.

"Just tell me. Please."

She opens the door, and the light from the hallway pours into her apartment.

"No, Nacio. You don't get to know the answer to that. I don't want to go to bed, worried that you are going to kill the father. We are through. And, if you do anything to change that, if you do anything to hurt me, my child, or the father…" Her voice trembles.

I involuntarily reach out to try to hold her. She lets me for a second, obviously just needing comfort from wherever she can get it. I hold her until she stops shaking. I smell the fresh, flowery scent in her hair from her shampoo. I study every curve of her body as she is pressed against me. I memorize the sound of her breathing, so I can take it with me forever to recall while I try to sleep.

I let her go without waiting for her to ask me to. Letting her go is the hardest thing I will ever do. And I'm not sure I will survive it. I'm not sure I'm strong enough.

"I love you, Beauty. I'm sorry it took me so long to figure it out, but I do. I never meant to hurt you. I just hope that the father takes care of you like you deserve."

I watch her drop her head. I see a tear sneak out from her eye and roll gently down her cheek. With one finger under her chin, I lift her head so that she is looking at me. And, looking at her, I know who the father is. There is only one other man it could be. Her ex. Jake.

I drove her back to him. I drove her to do something

stupid. I drove her to a lifetime of being stuck with that jerk. This is my fault.

"I'm sorry," I say with my own tears burning my eyes as I see how broken she is by what I've done to her.

"Me, too."

I close my eyes and lean my forehead against hers, wishing that things were different. If one or two things had been different, if I had just done things differently, she would have been mine right now. The baby would have been mine.

My heart speeds up at that thought. I'm not even scared at the thought of having a baby anymore. Not if a woman like Scarlett were there to take care of the baby with me. That will never happen now though.

I lean back. "I'm not going anywhere. If you need me, just call. No matter if it's just for a shoulder to cry on. No matter if that is all I can be for you."

She doesn't say anything. She just stares at me with her arms crossed over her chest, holding herself, trying to bring herself some comfort now that she is no longer in my arms and probably never will be again.

"I'm going to protect you. No matter what. You don't have to worry. I can at least give you that."

I turn my head to the brightly lit hallway and then look back at her one more time. I look at her in the darkness that she fits into so well. A darkness that I brought her into and taught her about. A darkness that welcomed her with open arms.

But she doesn't really belong in the darkness. She doesn't really belong with me. It was only meant to be a chapter of her life. A dark, dangerous chapter that she would tell her kids about when they were teenagers to explain the dangers of the world. It wasn't meant to be forever.

Now, it's my turn to step into the light. Not because the light will take me to her. Because I know it won't. It will just allow me to protect her in the way she deserves.

I take a step out into the lit hallway and don't look back.

"I'll protect you, Beauty. I love you, Beauty. No matter what."

2

SCARLETT

MY PHONE BUZZES with the alarm, startling me from a nightmare. The same nightmare I have every night. The nightmare that has become my reality.

The man I love is gone. He came to see me, and I just let him leave. No, I pushed him away and told him there was no chance of us being together. That we were over.

I told him the exact opposite of what I wanted to happen, but it was what had to happen. I can't be with him. Not now that a baby is involved. Not when so many people need my protection.

I roll over to grab my phone and turn off the alarm. I'm not getting out of bed today. I can't handle another day where he isn't in it. I don't see the point of getting out of bed. I roll back over, throwing the covers over my head to block out any light and the chill of the early morning.

I don't know why I set my alarm last night. It wasn't like I was actually going to go into work today. Last night, I felt defiant though. I felt like I could do anything. But, in the morning light, everything has changed because I didn't sleep for more than a couple of hours last night.

I take a couple of deep breaths, trying to get back to sleep, when my phone begins buzzing again.

I sigh. I must have hit the Snooze button instead of the Off button. I throw the covers off my head and grab my annoying phone off my nightstand, prepared to break it to get it to stop because I can't handle the shrill sound any longer.

I grab the phone and realize that the alarm isn't going off. Instead, Preston is calling me. I narrow my eyes at the phone as I read his name. I hit the Ignore button and then flop back down onto my bed. The phone rings again a second later.

I grab my forehead that is now pounding in pain with a headache.

On the third ring, I grab the phone and answer it with my eyes closed. "What?" I bark.

"Good morning, Scarlett. Just wanted to call and make sure you were up. I didn't want you to miss work again for the third time this week."

"I'm sick. I'm not coming in."

Preston laughs. "You don't get sick. I don't think, in the almost ten years I've worked for you, that you've ever called in sick, except this week. Even when you were nearly dying from the flu three years ago, you still came in until I convinced you to go see the doctor. And, even then, you didn't leave until after lunch. You're not sick. You sound fine."

"Well, I am sick. So, get over it, and just handle things, Preston."

"You're not sick. You're just depressed about that stupid guy. And you still haven't told me what happened with him."

"I'm sick. I'm not depressed about him. And don't expect

me to talk about him when you still haven't told me why you broke up with your girlfriend."

He pauses, and I think that maybe I've won. That he is going to let me sleep in. It's a Friday. No point in going in for one day and then not working all weekend. I would just have to start all over again on Monday. It'd be much better to just go in on Monday instead of starting off on Friday.

"You are coming in, Scarlett. Even if I have to come to your apartment and carry you into work myself. And I have a wedding I'm going to in California, so I would really like not to be sore or suffering from any broken bones because you know I'm not strong enough to carry even your light ass. So, don't make me come over there and do that because I will."

I sigh. Nothing he says is convincing me, but I am afraid that he is going to come here and drive me crazy until I come into work. I look around my messy bedroom. Clothes, pregnancy books, and leftover food are scattered throughout the room. I haven't told him yet that I'm pregnant, and I'm not ready to tell him today.

"Fine, I'm coming in. Don't get your panties in a bunch." I end the call just as a wave of nausea sets in.

I jump out of bed and run to my bathroom that is just off my bedroom. I make it just in time to empty my stomach into the toilet.

When my stomach finally seems to settle, I lean back against the wall, trying to catch my breath. I hate throwing up. It's the worst feeling. My doctor says it's a good sign. It means I will have a healthy baby, but it still isn't very reassuring. Not when I'll be dealing with my pregnancy symptoms alone—at least, for a little while longer. And it doesn't reassure me that I will have a healthy baby, not after my best friend lost her baby.

I go to the sink and wipe my face. I brush my teeth before I go back to my bedroom to find some clothes to wear. My phone buzzes, and I see a text message from Preston. He already let George, my driver, know to be ready to pick me up in half an hour.

I pull up George's number and ask him to pick me up some ginger ale and saltines. I'm going to need it to get through the day if I don't want to spend the whole day in the bathroom instead of working.

"You look like hell," Preston says with surprise as I walk into my office.

I run my hand through my hair that I washed, but didn't bother blow-drying or straightening. I know it's only a matter of time before it turns into a frizzy mess. I don't really care though. If I have any important meetings where I'll have to look better than this, I can have one of our stylists fix my messy hair.

"You didn't even put on any makeup," Preston says as he follows me into my office.

"Nope. I'm going for the fresh-faced look. Isn't that the style these days?"

"Well, yes, but in order to pull off the fresh, clean face, most women still wear some makeup. They just wear it in such a way so that it looks like they aren't wearing any makeup. You look like..."

"Death."

He nods.

"I told you, I'm sick. I don't feel well. So, can you please stop discussing how horrible I look and tell me what I absolutely have to do today so that I can get out of here as soon as possible?"

Preston nods and then places my latte on my desk. I pick up the drink, lifting it to my lips, but I know I can't drink it. I haven't drunk coffee in weeks—and not because caffeine isn't the best thing for the baby. I would love to drink some caffeine if it helped me get out of bed in the morning. For some reason, the baby—who I will question a lot in the future about torturing me so much while I was pregnant—doesn't like coffee and won't let me drink any without getting sick.

For the last couple of weeks when I have been in the office, I've waited until Preston has left before I pour the latte out, so he won't grow suspicious because, all of a sudden, after ten years, I no longer drink lattes.

My nose scrunches up at the smell, and I know I'm not going to be able to wait until he leaves. The smell alone is going to make me—

I run to the trash can in the corner of the room and dry-heave into it since nothing is left in my stomach. To my surprise, Preston runs over to me and rubs my back as I attempt to vomit.

It takes a moment for my stomach to settle before I sink onto the small couch in my office. Preston runs out of the room and returns with some ginger ale. It's the second one I've had today after George got me one this morning.

I take a sip. "Thanks."

Preston takes a seat next to me as I lean my head back against the headrest.

"I'm sorry. I didn't realize you were really sick. I thought you were just moping around because of that guy. And we have a meeting with Madeline, so I just thought—"

ELLA MILES

I sit up and look at Preston. "Wait, today is the meeting with Madeline, the amazing designer from France?"

Preston nods. "Yes, she flew in this morning and is in town for only a couple of hours. I know you wanted to meet with her and see if she would be interested in working with you on a children's line. I knew you wouldn't want to miss it, but I can see now that we will have to find a way to reschedule."

"No."

Preston narrows his eyes at me. "No? But you are sick, Scarlett. You can't possibly get through a meeting with her when you are likely to vomit all over her if she decides to bring in a coffee or any other food, which is likely since the meeting is supposed to be over lunch."

I glare at Preston. He's the one who called me into work today when I told him I couldn't make it, and now, he's trying to convince me that I shouldn't actually work after I dragged myself out of bed to come here. That's not happening. I'm taking the meeting, no matter what he says.

"I'm taking the meeting."

"No, you aren't. You're sick, Scarlett. I'm taking you to see a doctor. Then, I'm taking your butt to the nearest bed, and I'm not letting you leave until you feel a lot better."

I shake my head. "I'm not going to the doctor. I already know what I have. And I'm going to be fine."

I stand up to walk back to my desk. Preston stands as well, stepping between me and my desk. He pushes me back into a seated position.

"You are going to sit your ass down right there until I can make sure you have an appointment with your doctor, and then I'll get ahold of George to come pick you up."

I get a whiff of something. I think it is peanut butter on his breath, and I reach for the trash can, scared that I'm going to vomit again. I feel the uneasiness in my stomach grow as I try to deal with the offensive smell, but since nothing is left in my stomach, I don't actually throw up.

"See? You can't even sit here for a couple of minutes without getting sick."

"I didn't get sick," I say, glaring at Preston.

He rolls his eyes at me. "Close enough. Now, let's get you to the doctor," Preston says, standing in front of me with his hands outstretched to help me off the couch.

"Oh, for Christ's sake! I'm pregnant, Preston!"

Preston's eyes grow large, and he falls back onto the couch next to me.

"Whose baby is it?"

The question doesn't come from Preston sitting next to me. The voice comes from the male standing in my doorway. A man I know all too well.

I run my hand through my hair that is now more frizz than wet ringlets. I try to force a smile onto my lips, but it's no use. *How can I smile when I just told an ex I was pregnant after I'd planned on not telling anyone yet? Not even Preston.*

"Hi, Jake," I say, getting up from the couch. I walk over to my desk like I'm his boss and not his ex-girlfriend. "What can I help you with?" I ask, trying to shift the conversation from my pregnant belly that Jake is now staring at, despite it not changing shape yet, to work, the only thing I'm willing to talk about with Jake.

Jake takes a step into my office. I glance to the door. I don't remember if Preston closed it or not when we entered. I don't know if Jake just pushed into my office without knocking or if he just happened to be standing outside of my open door when I shouted out to the world that I was pregnant. I watch as Jake turns around and shuts the door, like that is going to help now.

Jake turns back to me. "Whose baby is it, Scarlett?"

I narrow my eyes at him. I can't believe he just asked me that again. I take a seat behind my desk without removing my eyes from his. "What do you need, Jake?"

He briskly walks forward and places his hands on my desk as he leans over, looking me square in the face. He's not happy. His cheeks are red, and his eyes darken as he looks at me. But he has no reason not to be happy with me. He's not my boyfriend anymore, not even my friend. He's just an employee that I can't wait to get rid of.

"I need to know who is responsible for knocking you up. I need to know so that I can make sure he is properly taking care of you."

I shake my head. "I can't believe you. You have no right to ask me that. It's none of your business. None." I take a deep breath, trying to remain calm. I don't know much, but I'm sure getting angry won't help the baby at all. "Now, if you don't have any work-related things to talk about, I think you should leave."

"Scarlett, just tell me. I want to help," Jake says.

"I don't need your help. All I need you to do is keep your mouth shut. I mean it. Not one word to anyone in this office. If I find out that people know, I'll blame you, and I will fire you so fast that you won't be able to get another job anywhere in the city. As far as you are concerned, I'm not pregnant. I'm not anything."

I can see the anger steaming off of Jake. His cheeks are redder than I've ever seen them, and his eyes are piercing through me, begging me to tell him the truth. But he doesn't get to know the truth yet. No one does.

Jake slowly removes his hands from my desk and stands up straight. "I'm here if you need me." He turns around and walks out the door.

I get up from my desk and quickly shut and lock my office door behind him. I don't need anyone else overhearing my conversation with Preston.

Preston—who has been quietly sitting on the couch, watching my exchange with Jake—gets up and walks over to me. He puts his arms around me and pulls me into a hug. A hug I didn't realize how much I desperately needed.

The hug doesn't last nearly long enough. Not long enough to wash away all the pain and despair I've been feeling. Just long enough to bring me enough comfort to get through the rest of my day.

"Congrats, Scarlett! I don't know how you feel about the baby, and it seems you aren't ready to share who the father is, but I know you'll be happy once the baby is here," Preston says as he lets go of me.

I smile and wipe a tear that found its way onto my cheek. "Thanks, Preston. I am excited about this baby. I know it's the best thing that has ever happened to me. And, no, I'm not ready to talk about whose baby it is yet. But thank you for being so supportive."

"And don't worry; I'll help keep your secret quiet, and I'll make sure Jake does the same."

I nod. "Thank you. That includes Kinsley, too, though. I'm not ready to tell her yet."

"Why?"

"After what she went through, I'm just not ready to tell her. I know she will be happy for me, but I don't want to cause her any pain."

Preston studies me for a second and then nods his understanding. "Of course. Whatever you want. Just know, I'm always here for you. Always."

I feel the tears coming again, but I can't handle any more crying today. "Good. Now, go get me some saltines and a ginger ale. Then, get someone to come up and do my hair and makeup so that I'm prepared for my meeting with Madeline."

Preston nods and then leaves.

I sigh, staring at the pile of work lying on my desk. I don't know how I ever managed to take a few days off to be with Nacio. There is just always too much work.

My stomach grumbles, and I place my hand over it. I still can't believe there is a baby inside me.

Albeit it is a teeny, tiny baby that is only a few weeks old, it's still a baby.

A baby that will be the redemption I need after all the horrible things I have done. A baby that will save me.

3

___

BEAST

"I'm picking you up," Santino says on the other end of the line.

"No," I say.

"I'm picking you up," Santino says again.

"No, I'm done. I don't want to have anything to do with the business anymore. Tell Reina I'm done."

Santino laughs. "I'm picking you up. Now. After all the shit you've put me through, you owe me."

He ends the call, and I toss my cell onto the couch cushion of my new black leather couch. A couch I bought along with all the other furniture in this expansive penthouse apartment that I recently bought after deciding to move here permanently. As long as Scarlett is in New York, this is my home. I can't stand being away from her. I can't stand being in a different city or state or country. I have to be here. So, I've finally settled down in an apartment after years of living in hotels. I finally have a permanent home that has nothing to do with my family or the business. Or my life before prison. Before I saw her. Before my whole life changed.

Except this apartment is anything but a home. It feels more like a prison. A cage where I am trapped and can't escape to go to her. Despite that being all I want to do.

But I don't want to leave and deal with Reina's or Santino's crap. I just want to sulk. I don't want to work. Because even working isn't going to bring me out of the darkness that has overcome me while I've been without her. And the only way to protect her is to stay away from everything in my past.

I hear three loud pounds against my front door. I know it's Santino, but I don't want to face him. I don't want to work, not today. Today, I want to finish the scotch that I poured for myself before Santino called. I want to drown my sorrows away until the pain from finding out that Scarlett is pregnant by another man is gone.

I hear Santino knock again, but I don't go to the door. Instead, I grab my glass of scotch and plop down on the couch. Nope, I'm not going anywhere today. I don't plan on going anywhere unless it is to see Scarlett or spy on her and make sure she is okay.

I take a sip of the scotch and enjoy the numbness that follows each sip of the amber-colored liquid. The pounding on the door stops, and I assume that Santino has given up. That he will leave me the fuck alone now. Something that I was very used to until Scarlett came into my life and showed me that being alone sucks. It's lonely and empty. It's not what I want.

I hear someone messing with the lock to my apartment. *Shit.* I run my hand through my hair, and then I take another sip of my scotch, knowing that this will be my last moment of peace and quiet before Santino breaks into my apartment.

I glance over at the door just as Santino breaks into my apartment.

"I told you, you are coming with me," Santino says.

"I told you, no," I say.

"And I told you, you don't get to tell me no," he says.

Santino storms over to me and snatches the scotch out of my hand. "Enough drinking. It's time to get to work," he says.

"No. I'm done working for her."

"You don't get to decide that. Only Reina decides when you can quit."

Santino carries the glass to my kitchen and sets it down on the counter next to the sink.

I get up off my ass, angry that he took away my scotch, the only thing that was holding me together these last couple of days. "Can't you handle the job on your own? Or are you really not capable of handling anything on your own?"

Santino frowns at me. "This is a two-man job."

"Sure it is."

I snatch the scotch off the kitchen counter and down the whole thing before he can protest. If I'm going to do this, I'm at least going to enjoy myself. Because I know he's not going to leave me alone until I agree to go with him. I slam the glass back down on the counter, sad that I wasted twenty-five-year-old scotch by downing it in one gulp.

"Let's go then. I want to get this over with, so I can get back to sulking, like I want."

Santino shakes his head at me and then begins walking toward the door of my apartment. I follow him out, and we take the elevator down to the garage level where my car is parked.

I climb into the driver's seat of my Mercedes, and Santino climbs into the seat next to me. I begin driving without asking him where I'm going. It doesn't matter. Every job is the same. Every job ends with death, suffering, and pain.

"So, what's the job anyway?" I ask.

Santino looks at his hands before he answers, "It's an easy job really. The guy's already dead. We just have to dispose of the body in such a way that it sets up his boss— some Callum guy."

I watch Santino out of the corner of my eye as I continue driving, still not having a clue as to where I'm going. He looks nervous, anxious. His hands are fidgeting in his lap, and he won't make eye contact with me. His normal joking manner is gone. Something is up, and it has nothing to do with this job that he brought me to help out with for God knows why. Because this job is simple, just like he said. Setting up a guy for killing another is easy. We've done it hundreds of times before. And, honestly, Santino is better at this kind of job than I am. So, there's another reason I'm involved in this. There's something he's not telling me.

"What the hell is going on?" I ask.

Santino abruptly looks up at me. "Nothing. Just wanted to get you out of your funk."

"I don't believe you. Something else is going on here. Why would Reina care so much if I helped you do this job or not?"

Santino sighs and grips the back of his neck, rubbing hard. "We are worried about you. We know Scarlett's pregnant, and from the amount of scotch on your breath, I'm guessing the baby is not yours."

"How the hell do you know that Scarlett's pregnant? Have you been spying on me?"

"Of course we have, Nacio! That's my second job, man—

to make sure you are okay. I know I am supposed to be equal to you in the company, another man who Reina hires to do her jobs. Let's get real though; that's not really my job. My job is to make sure that you, the perfect one, are okay, so you can do your job. Because everyone knows you're better at this than I am. You were born to do this, bred to do this, while I am just supposed to make sure you stay alive."

I feel my anger boiling inside me. I hate that Reina thinks she has to send Santino to watch out for me. And I hate that Santino doesn't think that he is just as capable of doing this job as I am. Because he is. The only difference is, what I've been through versus what he's been through. I'm messed up; he's not. That's why I'm better at this job than he is. If he'd experienced what I had been through, he would have been just as much of a killer as me.

I don't want to talk about this anymore. Despite the anger pulsing through my veins, I don't want to talk about Scarlett or Santino. I don't want to think about any of it because, if I'm distracted while doing this job, despite how easy it is, I'll fuck up and get caught. And I really can't take that chance right now. Not when I need to do everything in my power to protect the people I love.

"Where are we going?"

Santino curiously looks over at me, wondering about the sudden change in topic. But he doesn't question me about it.

"Long Island," he says.

I turn a hard right onto the next street to head in that direction. I don't stop driving until we've reached our destination.

I slam the ax down and watch as the left arm separates from the body. I watch the blood splatter onto the dirt ground. I've seen worse. Things that would make most men's stomachs churn. Not mine. Not my brother's. This is just daily life for us.

I drop the ax and begin putting the body parts into the garbage bags that Santino brought with us. Then, I make sure to place the hairs from Callum—the man we are setting up for the body I just dismembered—into the bags along with the parts. I scatter Callum's blood into the bags and on the ground to mix with the man's blood. I still don't know the man's name or why he died. And I don't care about either. Just like I don't care that I could be sending Callum, an innocent man, away to jail for a very long time. Although I doubt he is truly innocent. He might be innocent of this man's death, but everyone is guilty of something.

We leave nothing to chance as we plant the evidence for the police to find. We tie up the plastic bags and then toss them into the back of my car until the entire body is resting in the trunk. We gather up our things, the leftover trash bags and the ax. I wrap up the ax in a garbage bag before placing it next to the body parts in the trunk—things we will have to dispose of later—before climbing in the front seat.

I don't have to ask Santino where we are going to dump the body. I know we will dump the body anywhere along the shoreline to ensure that it washes up. This isn't one of the times when we want to kill someone and make them disappear. This is one of the times when we want to make sure that they are found. I drive a little ways from the warehouse where this man's body was originally dumped.

I park once I find a beach that isn't currently crowded,

but where I know the body will be quickly found come morning. Santino and I climb out, and I pop the trunk. From the shore, we make quick work of the body, tossing all the pieces into the water, not caring that his body won't even make it out to sea. We don't bother to stand and contemplate what we just did. Neither of us is affected by it. We just do our jobs and then quickly climb back into the car without so much as a glance in the rearview mirror.

I begin driving back to my apartment, and that's when I feel the anger coming back. Because doing the work without thinking or talking gave me time to realize why Reina had sent Santino to have me help him do this job. And it has everything to do with Scarlett.

"Reina sent you here to convince me to kill Kinsley, didn't she?"

Santino doesn't look at me, but he answers, "Yes."

My grip on the steering wheel is so hard that my knuckles begin turning white. "How could she think that I'd be able to kill Kinsley when I'm in love with Scarlett? How could she ask me to do that?"

Santino solemnly looks at me. "Because she still thinks you want revenge. For Kinsley sending you to jail and…"

I raise my eyebrows at him.

"And she thinks you want to hurt Scarlett now that she's hurt you."

"No way in hell! No way in hell am I going to do that! I don't want to hurt her. I want to protect her."

"Calm down! That's what I told her. I told her that you wouldn't want to do it. But she wouldn't listen to me. She never listens to me. She only ever listens to you."

"Well, tell her anyway. Tell her, no fucking way."

Santino nods. But I'm not satisfied with a nod. Not satisfied that Reina still wants me to kill Kinsley. That can't happen.

"You have to tell me what Reina is planning. I know she wants me to be the one to kill Kinsley. It sends a better message to our competition if one of the Marlows takes her out in revenge. But it's not going to be me. And it sure as hell is not going to be you."

Santino nods in agreement.

So, I continue, "But it can't be anyone else. No one touches her. Find out what Reina's plans are. I need you to find out who's going to do it and when it's going to happen, so I can stop it. Can you do that?"

Santino nods again.

"That's not good enough. I need to hear you say it."

"I can do that. Although I'm pretty sure, if Reina has anything planned, she'll tell you first."

That might have been true in the past, but it's no longer true now. Since Reina told me the truth, we are no longer the brother and sister we once were. She knows she no longer has me in her corner. So, she won't tell me anything.

4

SCARLETT

I TAKE a sip of my water as I sit in the booth of the Italian restaurant where Kinsley agreed to meet me. She's a little late, which I usually don't mind, except I'm starving today. After I've been sick for most of the morning, the baby has finally decided it's time to eat something. I'm thankful for that. I'm just not thankful that Kinsley is late. She's never really late. I'm the one who's always late.

The waitress comes back over with a smile on her face. "Can I get you anything else to drink or an appetizer to start? Or would you prefer to wait until your friend shows up?"

"How about you bring me some breadsticks? I'll just stick with water for now."

The waitress nods. "I'll be right back."

I pull out my phone to check and see if Kinsley texted me. However, when I check, there are no new messages. None. None from Kinsley. None from Nacio. Not even any messages from Preston about work.

I sigh and then sip on my water, but it does nothing to

quench my hunger or thirst. I stare at the door of the cute little Italian restaurant we chose to meet for dinner. Killian is working tonight, and I haven't seen Kinsley in a couple of weeks. And I know she's anxious to see me.

My fingers drum along the table as I wait for Kinsley— or at least for my breadsticks to appear. Finally, after what seems like hours, the waitress finally brings me a basket of three breadsticks. I pull the first one out of the basket and quickly eat it without setting it down. And then I pull the second one out of the basket and make quick work of it before Kinsley finally arrives.

"I'm so sorry, Scar! Traffic was a nightmare, and Killian decided to sneak home for an hour before he had to go back in for some meetings," Kinsley says, winking at me. She leans over to give me a quick hug and then takes a seat in the booth opposite me.

I smile at my friend across the booth. "It's not a problem at all. I figured something like that happened."

Our waitress quickly finds her way back to our booth and says, "Can I get you anything to drink?"

"Yes! I'm in desperate need of wine. Scar, will you share a bottle of white wine with me?"

"Oh, I don't think so. I drank too much last night, and I'm still a bit hungover. You go ahead though."

"Since when do you not drink?" She turns her attention to the waitress. "Bring us a bottle of your best white wine. Something sweet."

"Certainly. I'll be right back with the wine and to take your order," the waitress says before leaving.

"Kinsley, I'm really not in the mood for any alcohol. I've still got a splitting headache and a queasy stomach."

"Exactly why you need a little bit of alcohol. It will do you good."

I sigh and take another sip of water, trying to figure out how I can get out of not drinking without telling her I'm pregnant. I want to tell her. I'm dying to tell her, but I'm just not ready yet.

I snatch up the third breadstick from the basket and start absentmindedly eating it, not even thinking about how it might look.

Suddenly, Kinsley squeals, "Oh my God! You're pregnant!"

I slowly swallow the breadstick in my mouth as I try to figure out what I'm going to say. I open my mouth, but no words come out.

"I knew that was why you wanted to have dinner with me tonight. I knew it!"

"I'm not pregnant," I say nonchalantly while rolling my eyes, like she's crazy.

"Yes, you are."

"No, I'm not," I lie through my teeth.

The waitress comes back with our bottle of wine, temporarily halting our conversation. Kinsley tastes the wine that was chosen, and after she approves, the waitress pours us each a glass of white wine.

"Are you guys ready to order?"

"Yes, I'll have the lasagna," I say.

"And I'll have the spaghetti," Kinsley says.

"Anything else? Soup or salad or another appetizer to begin with?"

I take my time thinking, trying to come up with something else to order, something else to keep Kinsley from asking me more questions, like if I am pregnant or not. I'm not ready to tell her that I am. I don't want to hurt her. I don't want to get her hopes up and then have to go through the pain with me if I lose this baby like she lost hers. Better to keep it to myself until I'm farther along.

Kinsley smiles, like she's somehow read my thoughts. "No. Just the pasta will be fine."

The waitress walks away.

"So, you're not pregnant?" Kinsley asks with a smug smile on her face.

"Nope, not pregnant. Just like I told you before."

"Then, prove it." Kinsley nods in the direction of the wine sitting in front of me.

I lift the glass of wine to my lips and take a drink as nonchalantly as I can. And then I swallow. I know one sip of wine isn't going to do anything to harm the baby. In fact, my doctor even said it was okay to have an occasional glass of wine. Although I have never had a drop of alcohol since finding out I was pregnant.

"Satisfied now?" I ask.

Kinsley takes a drink of her own wine as she stares intensely at me. "No, but it will do for now."

"So, how are you and Killian doing? Anything new?"

"Not really. We are planning on going to Mexico next week just to give ourselves a little bit of a getaway."

"That'll be fun," I say.

Kinsley takes another sip of her wine, thinking deeply. "Yeah, it will be. I'm just not sure if a vacation is going to be enough to bring me out of my depression over losing Wesley. I know it's been months since we lost him, but it's still hard. For me, it still feels like yesterday."

"I understand. You guys just need to do whatever you can to try to heal. It's not going to be easy, but you will get there eventually."

Kinsley smiles and nods as she lifts her glass of wine to

her lips again, drinking until her glass is only half-full. Her eyes go to my wine glass that is still completely full.

Damn it! How am I going to get out of this?

I lift my own glass of wine to my lips and pour some of the liquid into my mouth. I don't want to swallow any more of the alcohol. I know it's not great for the baby, and if I drink more alcohol, I'm sure I'm going to be sick. I put the wine glass back down, still holding the liquid in my mouth, when I remember my water glass. I pick up the water and touch the glass to my lips, slowly letting the liquid pour into my water glass. The glass is opaque, so it's hard to see exactly how much liquid is in it. I'm thankful that Kinsley ordered white wine instead of red.

"Work is going well. Nothing new to report really," I say.

Kinsley sips on her wine again, so I do the same, forcing the sweet liquid into my mouth and then out again into my water glass.

"Have you met any new guys lately?" Kinsley asks, wiggling her eyebrows at me.

"No. I haven't really been thinking about guys lately. Just focusing on my work, you know."

Kinsley nods, but from the smile on her face, I can tell that she doesn't believe me. *I don't care. Let her think what she wants about me.*

The waitress brings our food, and I dig in right away, not caring that the boiling hot cheese is burning my tongue as I eat my lasagna. I'm starving.

We continue our meal together, going back and forth about how our jobs are going and things we want to do. We continue eating. I'm laughing and talking and drinking until we are each on our last glass of wine. Mine has mostly been used to refill my water glass although I will admit that I drank an occasional sip or two.

"I'm going to use the restroom," Kinsley says, getting up from the booth.

I nod and watch as she walks to the restroom. Then, I quickly flag down our waitress.

She walks over and then asks casually, "Can I get you anything?"

"Yes. Can you get me a new glass of water?" I hand her my glass filled with wine.

She takes that away and quickly comes back with my glass of water. As soon as she brings it, I drink half of the glass of water, thankful to finally be able to drink something to get the taste of white wine out of my mouth.

Kinsley returns from the restroom, takes a seat in the booth, and we each leave some cash on the table to pay for our bill.

"Are you ready to go?" I ask.

"Almost," she says with a sly smile on her face.

I quizzically look at her. "Almost?"

Before I realize what Kinsley is doing, she grabs my glass of water and takes a sip.

I stand, watching her, with my arms folded over my chest. After she finally determines that my glass of water is in fact water, she sets it down on the table with a frown on her face. She quickly gets up from the booth.

I follow her and stop her before she makes it to the door of the restaurant. "What was that about?"

"Sorry. I just thought you were pregnant and that you were slipping the wine into your water glass. I guess I was wrong."

I grab my friend and wrap her in a tight hug. "It will happen. One of these days, it will happen for one of us. And, when it does, it will be amazing. Because that child is going to have love from both of us, no matter whose it biologically is."

And, even though that day is now, I can't tell her. It would break her heart if something happened to this baby. She wouldn't survive. And, if she didn't, I wouldn't either.

5

SCARLETT

I CLIMB into the car as George, my driver, holds the door open for me. He shuts the door after I get in, and he quickly makes his way to the driver's seat.

As he begins driving me back to my apartment, I sulk in the fact that I just lied to my best friend. I hated doing it, but it was necessary at this point. I need to wait until the pregnancy is much further along and I know I'm as safe as I can be before I tell her. If I lose the baby after she lost hers only months ago, it will destroy her. I don't think she will survive that kind of heartbreak. And I don't think I'm strong enough to do that to her or to get her through the heartbreak. I'm not sure if even Killian would be strong enough to get her through that.

I go through my messages on my phone, trying to distract myself, but I have no text messages again. I go through my emails, all one hundred seven of them, and begin typing out quick responses. I get through about twenty before George pulls up in front of my apartment. I sigh. Looks like I'll be spending the rest of my night answering emails.

George opens my door, and I climb out.

"Thanks," I say, trying to keep a smile on my face so that George doesn't grow suspicious.

I'm pretty sure though that George already knows I'm pregnant. After the doctor visits and the late-night runs to get me crackers, Sprite, or ice cream, he must at least have his suspicions. George is a good man though. I'm not at all concerned that he will mention this to anybody.

"Have a good night, Miss Bell. I'll be on call. If you need anything tonight, just let me know."

I smile. "You're the best, George."

He nods and watches me walk into my apartment building, like he always does.

"You didn't tell her," a voice says next to me.

It's a voice that I recognize all too well.

"What are you doing?" I ask as I stand frozen with my hand on the door that leads into my apartment building.

"Why didn't you tell her?" Nacio asks against my ear, ignoring my question.

I turn and face him as my heart stops. He's gorgeous, standing next to me, in his jeans and T-shirt that fit his muscles all too well. Every bit of him begs me to take him back, to just forget about everything and start over with him.

Somehow, I gather the strength to ignore him. I push the door open and walk into my apartment building. I don't wait to see if he is following me or not. I want him to stay the hell away. Stay away so that my life is safe and happy and makes sense. But, on the other hand, I want him to follow me, to come up to my apartment, to not take no for an answer. And the second feeling is the one I'm worried about. It's the one that might get me in trouble.

I climb onto the elevator and push the button to my

floor. I watch as the elevator doors close without Nacio. He didn't follow me. I breathe a sigh of relief, but I also feel my anxiety growing. My heart is beating fast. I ready myself for the pain that is about to come, knowing that I'm not going to get to spend time with him today, that I'm not going to get to spend time with him ever. And that kills me.

The elevator seems to be moving in slow motion as it rises higher and higher until it reaches my floor. I step off the elevator, and I walk toward my apartment door. Then, I can't help myself as I grin when I see Nacio leaning against my door. I don't know how in the hell he beat me up here, but right now, I don't care. I'm happy to see him. Way too happy to see him.

"I'm surprised you haven't already broken into my apartment," I say.

He grins. "I'm trying to be good."

I walk to the door and feel my hand brush against his for just a split second before I insert the key into the lock. "You call this being good?"

He nods slowly.

"You call following me to the restaurant and then spying on a private conversation good? Because I call it stalking." I push the door open and hope that he's going to follow me inside without being invited.

I walk straight to my kitchen and grab the gin from my bar. I begin pouring myself a glass before I realize that I can't drink. "Shit," I curse when I run my hand through my hair. I take the glass and pour it down the drain.

I glance up and see him watching me with the same eyes that Kinsley was watching me with before. Trying to decide what the truth is or not. To see if I'm just pretending like I can't drink or if I really can't because I'm pregnant.

But, unlike Kinsley, I can't tell if he believes me or not.

His face is too hard for me to read. Despite knowing every line on his chiseled face, every muscle, every face this man makes, I don't know him well enough to know if he believes me or not.

"Why didn't you tell her that you are pregnant?" Nacio asks.

He takes a step forward and then another until we are standing face-to-face. He reaches out and tucks a strand of hair behind my ear. "If you're really pregnant, then why didn't you tell your best friend?"

"Because I don't want to break her heart if something happens and I lose this baby," I answer honestly, not really sure why I'm telling him the truth. Not sure why I can lie to my best friend but not to this man.

"And Kinsley finding out that you lost your baby would break her heart?"

I nod. "Yes, it would. I know most people wouldn't understand that, but Kinsley and I are close. We are connected in ways that most people don't understand."

Nacio studies me again with his piercing eyes and unreadable expression.

I have a hard time breathing as he stares at me. I hate how easily he can affect me. I hate that, despite knowing all he's done—the killings, the abuse, the lies—I would still let him flip me over and take me right here on my kitchen counter if he wanted to. And, from the way he's looking at me now, it makes me think that is exactly what he wants to do. I let him know that is what I want, as I bite my lip, waiting to see what he will do.

I'm quickly disappointed when he takes a step back instead of kissing me like I want him to do. Instead of throwing me over the counter and doing dirty, nasty things to me to make me forget all the reasons we can't be together.

"I didn't come here to just ask you that question. I need to talk to you," he says, turning away from me and walking toward my living room.

I take a second to catch my breath, and then I follow Nacio into my living room. He takes a seat on the couch, and I take a seat next to him, waiting for him to tell me whatever he came here to tell me. Whatever he came here to tell me doesn't come easily for him. I try to be patient as I wait for Nacio to talk. And I don't know if it's because I'm tired, just tired of dealing with all the lies, or if it's the pregnancy hormones, but I lose all my patience.

"Just tell me already. Whatever it is, it can't be worse than what I already know about you."

Nacio looks at me with such sadness in his eyes, and I'm afraid that it might be much worse than what I thought.

He instantly gets up from the couch and begins pacing the room. He walks back and forth, and I try to remain calm by counting his steps.

One, two, three, four...

And so on and so forth until I lose count somewhere around two hundred.

He runs his hand through his hair and then grabs his neck before he finally stops and looks at me.

"Everything Reina told you was a lie," Nacio slowly says, staring at me with such intensity, such hope, that I realize he must be telling the truth. There is no way someone could say words like that with such meaning behind them if they weren't true.

"How...how is that possible? So, you lied to me earlier when you told me that her words were true?"

"No."

I stand, trying to understand his confusing words, and I

find myself pacing just as he was before as I try to make sense of what he's saying or not really saying.

Nacio stares at me in silence as I pace back and forth, and I assume he's counting my steps just like I was earlier. *What else could be going through his head?*

I finally stop and look at him. "Explain."

"At the time, I thought everything that Reina told you was true. I thought that I had abused her when we were younger. I thought I had destroyed her life. I thought I was a monster and born to be a killer. But it's not true."

I watch as he takes a deep breath in and out, as if he is still trying to come to terms with it himself.

"But what I didn't realize was that, even though I had done all those things, I had been abused, just like Reina. My father was the one who had made me do those things. I'd only abused her because my father forced me to."

I can see the pain and the demons that haunt him in his eyes. His entire life, he thought that he'd hurt his sister. That he was the one who had destroyed her life. In reality, he was only a child who had been just as abused as she was.

I move to him and wrap him in my arms. I hold him while I try to take the pain away. I feel his body shake, and I know he's crying. I hold him tighter, letting him know it's okay to cry, to feel the pain, to feel everything. And, to my surprise, he opens up and cries harder.

I don't know how long we stand there, just holding each other, but it's long enough that I cry, too. I cry for the boy who was abused and, in turn, forced to appease another. I cry for the young man who thought he was a monster. I cry for the man I'm holding in my arms who is forced to relive everything.

When I know we can't cry any longer, I pull his buried face from my shoulder and look at him.

I see him for the first time. Not as a killer. Not as Nacio. Not even as Beast.

Just as a man.

A man who has feelings and dreams and desires, just like all the rest of us. A man who deserves love. Love that I want to give him.

I don't know how it happens, but my lips slowly lower to his. It's a slow, gentle kiss. I rationalize it as a sweet, innocent kiss and nothing more. But my sweet kiss soon turns to fire as Nacio grabs the sides of my face with his hands. He firmly holds me to him as his tongue slips forcefully between my lips.

I moan; I can't help myself. I've denied myself this feeling for months now.

And what will a couple of innocent kisses hurt?

I kiss him back as my hands go around his neck, needing him to be closer to me, needing more, but there is no way our bodies can get any closer. Our tongues are already buried inside each other's mouths, our lips are locked so tightly that both of us can barely breathe, and our hands are grasping on to each other as our bodies are pressed tightly together.

At the same time, we each realize that the only way to get closer together is to remove the clothing separating us. We start undressing each other. I grab for the hem of his black T-shirt and pull it off over his head. He grabs for the hem of my halter top and pulls it over my head. For that split second, our lips part, and clarity forms in my head. His mouth moves to cover mine again, but I put a hand up to stop him.

"I can't." I can't look at him as I say it because I know the pain I'll see there, and if I see it, I'll give in. I'll give in to letting him kiss me again. If I give in, I know, soon, we will be completely undressed and having sex before my mind clears again.

"I understand."

I look up because I wasn't expecting that response from him. "You do?"

"Yes," he says with such sadness in his eyes. "I understand that you still see me as a killer, a monster, as Beast. I know it will take some time for you to truly believe me."

I reach out and touch this broken man. "That's not why. I believe you. I believe that you're not a killer, a monster, or Beast."

"Then, why?"

"Because I realized, since coming back to my life, that we aren't right for each other, good for each other. Despite not being a killer or a monster, you will still want to kill for a living. And, despite me being more than just Beauty, I will still want to run a fashion empire and do more good in the world. How can those two worlds ever coexist?"

"They can't," he says.

I nod as a tear escapes, but he can't leave, just feeling pain. We have to feel *more*. We have to feel some tiny bit of happiness before I can let him leave again.

I kiss him. It's tentative, as I'm not sure that I should really be doing this, but I'm doing it all the same. And then, within a matter of seconds, it becomes so much more. It becomes what we both need in this moment. Comfort, happiness, love.

And then the kiss turns desperate. Desperate for more than we can give each other.

We kiss like it could be our last kiss with each other, desperately clinging on to one another. I grab ahold of his hair, desperately holding on to him. He grabs my waist, promising never to let me go. We know that promise he silently gives me with his body is a lie. We know that, despite how much we need to be together in this moment, it can never last. It can never be more than just a moment.

Nacio accepts this reality before I do. Gently, tentatively, he pulls away, and the pain I see left in his eyes equally matches my own.

"You won't let me fuck you like I want to. You won't let me take your pain away or let me show you how much I love you, but..." He pauses for a second and then gives me a dirty smile. "Will you let me watch you pleasure yourself while I do the same?"

I know his words are meant to be a question, but it's not; it's a command.

I bite my lip for a second as I consider his request. "Yes. That's exactly what I want."

He grins, and I about come just from the sexy smirk on his face, which only makes him grin wider.

"Undress for me, Beauty. Or would you prefer I do that for you?"

I watch as his eyes land on my bra and the jeans I'm still wearing. I know letting him undress me might be tempting us too far, but I don't care. I need his hands on me at least one more time.

"You," is all I can get out.

His grin turns serious now as he walks back to me and then steps behind me. A serious look for a serious task. If he lets himself lose control, we will wind up doing something that, although we will enjoy it in the moment, will destroy us in the end.

I feel his hands on my hips, and then they slowly slide around to the front. I close my eyes and ball my hands into fists to keep myself in control, to stop myself from turning around and throwing my body against his. His hands move to the button on my jeans, and he slowly undoes it, followed by lowering the zipper. Then, his hands are back at my hips, slowly moving the material down over my ass and then further down my body until my jeans are lying in a heap on the floor around my ankles. He kneels in front of me before he slowly lifts one of my ankles to remove one of my black pumps, followed by one side of my jeans. He is careful with where he places his hands, making sure not to tempt us any further by touching me anywhere but where he has to, to remove my clothing. He does the same to my other leg. As much as I want him to kiss my smooth, toned legs, he doesn't.

I feel his hands move back up my body to my bra. He undoes the clasp and then removes the straps from my shoulders until the bra falls on the floor, releasing my breasts. I suck in air as the cold air hits my nipples. I wait for his hands to go to my breasts, to touch me, but they don't.

"Touch them," he commands in my ear.

I suck in a second breath, but don't do as he said.

"Touch your breasts like I would. I know you want to."

I can't resist. I move my hands from my sides to my breasts. Keeping my eyes closed, I massage them like he would. I grab them and then run my thumbs across my nipples that are beyond hard. As I do so, I lose track of where his hands are, and I soon find that he is slipping my panties to the floor. I step out of them.

And then his hands are off me.

I open my eyes, searching for him, for some sort of connection now that his hands are no longer on my body. I find him staring at me with the same serious expression as before. My eyes trail over his body, from his naked torso to his jeans. Then, I come to a stop at his bulge.

I glance back up to his eyes, silently asking him the same question that he asked me, *Do you want me to undress you?*

He nods.

I walk over to him, and instead of standing in front of him, I kneel. He doesn't close his eyes like I did. Instead, he watches me. I take my hands and run them up the sides of his body until I reach the top of his jeans. My hand slides over to find the button. I slowly unbutton it, followed by lowering the zipper. He kicks off his shoes, and then I slide his jeans as I stare at him from where I'm still kneeling on the floor. My hands move back up to the waistband of his briefs, and I begin pulling slowly until I release the hard bulge hiding beneath. I don't watch as his underwear falls to the floor. Instead, my eyes are locked on his cock that has just sprung free.

"Like what you see?" he asks with a smug grin.

I bite my lip since no words can come out. Then, I look up at him with my big eyes, showing him how much I want to take it into my mouth but can't.

"Touch yourself," he says.

I respond automatically as I throb, needing to be touched. I slide my hand between my legs, between the folds, and rub slowly, spreading my juices over my pussy. The whole time, I never take my eyes off of his. I watch as he struggles to keep his hands off my body as I touch myself. I can see him beginning to lose control. I see the desire and lust in his eyes. His hands are shaking, begging to touch me, to fist my hair, to stroke me, anything.

But, instead, he grabs ahold of his cock and begins pumping as he watches me.

I struggle with deciding if I should keep my eyes on him or his cock. My eyes keep going back and forth, up and down, trying not to miss a moment of how his hand is wrapped around his cock or his expression as he looks at me while I pleasure myself.

As we touch ourselves, we struggle to breathe or move at the same time, and I know we are both close. I can't take it much longer when he looks at me with such intensity. I come about a second before him and then watch as he comes all over my breasts.

When we have each finished, we collapse onto the rug on the floor. Neither of us says a word. Neither of us has to because we know what the other is thinking—how that was exactly what we needed, but we will never get enough.

I drift in and out of sleep, lying on the floor for a long time, until I finally decide to get up. "I'm going to go take a shower." I head upstairs toward my bedroom without waiting for an answer, a good-bye, or a word.

And, after my shower, when I make my way back downstairs in a tank top and pajama pants, he's gone.

6
___

BEAST

I STEP out of the shower in my own apartment, feeling emptier than ever.

I went to see Scarlett. I thought, if I told her the truth, she would want to be with me, despite everything that was going on. I was wrong.

Instead, she told me that I couldn't change. She told me that, although she didn't think of me as a killer or monster or Beast, it was still what I would always want to do for a living, that there would always be this desire in me to do just that.

I look at myself in the mirror. Maybe she's right. Because all I see when I look at myself is a killer. And that's not good enough for her. I don't deserve her love or to be around for her baby if that's all I am.

I need to change. I need to be someone else. I just don't know who that is yet.

All I've ever known is how to be a killer.

I walk back into my bedroom and get dressed, not having a clue what to do. I have plenty of money, so that's not a concern. If I know Scarlett, she doesn't care if I ever work another day in my life because, between the two of us, we have more money than we would ever need.

But I need to find some purpose in life, something to show her that I've truly changed my path, but it's not going to be volunteering or doing some job that saves the world and all that crap. That's not me.

I just don't know who I am beyond a killer.

My phone vibrates on my nightstand, and I walk over and pick it up. The number on the screen is unknown. But I know exactly who it is—my other employers, who are more demanding than Reina. They are bigger monsters than us all. I wouldn't put up with their crap, but the pay is better than what Reina can offer.

I answer the phone, "Hello?"

"Do you have anything for us?" Elliot, my boss, asks.

"Not yet, but I'm on it. You'll know soon enough."

"That's not good enough! We need that info now. You are losing our trust, and you need to get it back before we rescind your deal."

I pace back and forth as I speak, "Not going to happen. That wasn't part of the deal. I don't have any new info for you. And, if you keep pressuring me, I'll quit, and then you'll have nothing."

"Calm down, calm down. Let's all play nice here. Neither of us wants that to happen, but you have to work with us a little bit, give us some information. The more defensive you get, the more we think you're lying. We are all on the same side here."

"You need to learn to trust me." I hang up the phone before he can argue back.

I'm tired of being everybody's puppet. I've always been Reina's and Santino's, and now, I'm Elliot's. I'm done. I should quit both jobs.

All I care about is keeping Scarlett safe. That's who I am —a protector. I'll make damn sure that no one hurts her or my family or anyone else.

I don't know how to show that to Scarlett or if she would even believe that's what I am. But I do know, from our conversation earlier today, that she is beginning to lose all control when it comes to saying no to me. And it won't take much for her to start saying yes a whole lot more.

So, that's what I have to do—prove to her that I'm more than just a killer. That I can be a nice guy, a caring guy, a loving guy. Prove to her that I can be her protector.

Because that's exactly what she needs—to be protected.

7

SCARLETT

I HEAR a knock on the door just as I finish blow-drying my hair. I run down the stairs to the door, hoping it is Nacio. But I already know it's not him. As I approach the door, I don't feel the spark of excitement that I usually do whenever he is close. When I open it, a doorman is standing there with the largest bouquet of roses I've ever seen.

"These are for you," he says with a smile on his face.

I look at him in confusion. "Are you sure? I don't have a boyfriend or husband or anything."

The doorman smiles wide. "I'm pretty sure. Are you Miss Scarlett Bell?"

I nod.

"Then, these are for you. Where would you like them?"

"I'll just take them from you," I say, reaching out my arms to take the large vase.

The doorman just smiles. "It's not just these flowers, ma'am. There are also at least a dozen more right behind me."

I pop my head outside my door and see half a dozen men, each one holding two vases in their hands. My jaw drops as I look at them. "Just bring them inside and put them in the kitchen or living room or wherever you can find a place for them."

I move out of the way and hold the door as the men begin carrying flowers inside before setting them all around my apartment. I watch as the men slowly leave, and then I go over to one and pick up an envelope. I open it and read.

DEAR BEAUTY,

I HAVEN'T GIVEN up on us yet. I know that Beauty and the Beast get together, but that's just a fantasy, just a movie, a story. It's not real life. But I want to make it real life. And I don't want anything to stand in the way of that.

I'm slowly figuring out who I am and how we can fit together. I don't have it all figured out yet, but in the meantime, I thought I could do something to at least bring a smile to your face. You've done the same to me from the second I saw you when I went away to jail ten years ago.

These flowers aren't enough, but they're a start.

LOVE,
Beast

I walk into my office at Beautifully Bell and stop dead in my tracks. My office is covered with flowers—roses, daisies, and several exotic flowers that I don't know the names of.

Every flower imaginable is covering every surface in my office. I can't even see my desk because it's covered with large bouquets. I can't see the floor because rose petals are everywhere. Even my couch has flowers draped across it.

I tiptoe into my office, careful not to disturb any of the flowers or petals on the floor, as if it would cause a bomb to explode. I finally make it to my desk and carefully sit down in my chair as I look around the room, trying to understand what Nacio thinks he's doing with sending me all these flowers. I've been sent flowers before but nothing like this. Nothing this extravagant or over the top.

I jump when Preston enters my office without knocking. "These from him?"

I look at Preston with confusion, as I'm not sure whom he's referring to. *Nacio? Jake? Or the baby's father?*

"It depends on what you mean by *him*. If you're referring to Nacio, then yes."

I begin trying to move the vases of flowers around on my desk so that I can get to my computer, but I soon realize it's no use. Once I pick up the first vase, I can't find another place for it on my desk. I guess they're all going on the floor, which is a shame since they are so beautiful. But it has to be done. So, I lift the first vase again and place it on the floor, followed by another.

"Here, let me help," Preston says, walking over to my desk.

"Thanks," I say.

"Nacio really sent you all these flowers?" Preston asks with a knowing smile on his face. "He doesn't happen to be..."

I roll my eyes. "I already told you. I'm not ready to tell you who the father is yet."

He shrugs. "Had to try."

"Just help me get all these flowers arranged somewhere, so I can actually get some work done today."

"And, if anyone asks, who am I supposed to say all these flowers are from?"

"Just say they are from you."

Preston raises his eyebrows at me. "Nobody's going to believe that I sent you these flowers."

"Sure they will. Just tell them you've noticed I've been feeling down lately, so you wanted to do something to cheer me up."

"I still don't think anyone's going to believe me, but I'll spread the lie around anyway."

"Thanks," I say as I place the last vase of flowers onto the floor. I'm not sure if it'll really work either, but it's the only option I have.

And it's not like Nacio's going to send me anything else. It's just for today.

Except it wasn't just for one day. It was for an entire week.

Every day this week, Nacio sent me something to my apartment, followed by more things to my office. He sent enough chocolate for everyone in my office to have a piece, cupcakes in the shape of a heart, and art pieces that are now covering my office walls. Today, the theme must be jewelry.

When I walk into my office, not as many items are covering my desk as there have been the last few days. Instead, only five boxes are sitting on my desk. And, without looking inside any of the boxes, I know he spent a lot more money today than he did on any of the items this past week.

Because the jewelry that he sent to my house was nice, nicer than anything I'd ever bought for myself—and I like diamonds and have money. I wouldn't be surprised if all these diamonds and jewelry combined cost him at least a million dollars. And I don't want to know how he earned the money to afford all these things.

At least this time, I will be able to hide his gifts. I quickly grab all the boxes and shove them into my desk drawer. I take my key from my purse, prepared to lock them away before anyone else gets the chance to see what he sent me. Before anyone gets a chance to question who the gifts are from and who my new boyfriend is.

After the first day, no one believed the story that Preston had sent me all the items. I spent the rest of the week dodging questions from everyone in my office and rumors about who my new mystery boyfriend could be. Jake is the obvious conclusion that most people have come to. That we are back together. Although there are even rumors that Preston and I have been hooking up. That would never happen.

I put the key in the lock on my desk, ready to lock them all away, but I freeze. I can't lock them all away without at least peeking. I glance at what Nacio bought me. Now, I'm regretting not wearing at least one of the pieces of jewelry that he sent to my apartment into work today. I knew that wearing something like that would incite more rumors, so I didn't, but it still didn't prevent me from wanting to.

Here's my second chance. I pull the drawer back open and take the last box back out of the desk. I hold it in my hands, but I don't open it. The second that I do, I'll want to wear it, and I'll fall even more in love with him for giving it to me.

But I can't stand just holding it in my hands. I open the

box and see the most beautiful ruby ring that I've ever seen. It's a large oval-shaped ruby with tiny diamonds that go all the way around the band. It's perfect for me. *If this man has such good taste in jewelry, I wonder what an engagement ring from him would look like.*

I shake my head. That can never happen.

I take the ring out of the box to get a closer look and then somehow find it on the ring finger of my right hand. I don't know how he knew what size ring to get me, but he did.

I hear a knock at the door, and I startle, slamming the box shut and tossing it into the open drawer. Closing it quickly, I flick the lock on the desk before I finally look at who's standing in my doorway.

Jake.

I can't even muster a fake smile as I look at him.

Once the rumors started to spread, he made it his mission to find a reason to stop by my office every day this week. Every time, he made up an excuse. It's always been work-related, but I know that's not why he is here. He is here to try to figure out who his competition is.

"What do you want, Jake?"

He smiles and takes a seat in front of me. "It must be a good sign if you are already locking my gifts away so that no one can steal them."

Fear takes over at his words. I try to think if I saw a note attached to the boxes, anything that would indicate who the jewelry was from. I don't remember a note being attached. I don't remember any indication that the jewelry was from Nacio and not Jake. I just assumed it was from Nacio since he was the one who had been sending me gifts all week. I never thought the gifts could be from anyone else.

"Good. I thought you would like it," he says with a smug smile as he studies the ring on my right hand.

My panic rises as I realize Jake got me this gorgeous ring. This ring that I had such a connection with and instantly felt a connection for the man who had given it to me, but now, I feel torn. I didn't fall in love with Nacio because he bought me this beautiful ring or any of the other gifts.

It doesn't matter anyway. I can't be with either of these men for the same reasons as before. Jake is a douche bag. And Nacio is Beast. Neither of them can give me what I truly want.

"Is that all?" I fold my arms across my chest and then lean back in my chair, hiding the ring from his view.

Whether it was from him or not, he doesn't need to know how I feel about it.

"I want to do more for you than just buy you nice jewelry. I want to help you. If he would quit sending you stupid gifts, like flowers and chocolate, then I could help. None of that shit is worthy of you. Let me help you. I would make a great father to your baby. Just give me a chance."

"No."

Jake ignores my no and begins walking around to the other side of my desk so that he is standing inches from me. I turn in my chair to glare at him, trying to get him to leave, to understand that he and I will never be an item. And, if he's not careful, I'll fire his ass right now instead of waiting until his contract is over.

He doesn't take the hint.

"Let me take you out tonight. Prove that you're wrong. Prove that I'm the man for you, that you need me to help you take care of this baby, Scarlett. You can't do this alone, not after how you were with my niece and nephew. You don't know how to handle children. Let me help you."

I thought this man had made me mad before, but I was wrong. I've never felt so much anger in all my life as I do right now.

"Get out of my office!" I scream at him, not even bothering to talk reasonably with him after he just said I would make a terrible mother. That I wouldn't be able to do this on my own.

Jake doesn't budge. He just stares at me, like he can't believe that I have any reason to kick him out.

So, I say firmly, "Get out of my office now."

He slightly steps back but still doesn't get out of my office like I asked. I pick up my phone and begin dialing Preston, prepared to call security or the police if I have to. Anything to get this man out of my office and my life forever.

"I want you out now, and if you don't leave, I'll call my security team. I also recommend that you start looking for other employment."

I am almost finished dialing when I hear Nacio say, "Are you ready for our date? If we don't leave now, we will be late for our dinner reservation."

I glance up and meet Nacio's eyes. I smile at him, thankful that he is standing in my doorway, even though I have no idea why he is here. "Yes. I was just finishing up a meeting."

I slip on my shoes and sling my purse over my shoulder as I brush past Jake. Nacio meets me halfway and takes me into a deep, passionate kiss, like he just came back from war or something. My mind is blank of everything but the kiss until Nacio lets me back up for air with a wide smirk on his face. It takes a second for enough air to return to my lungs. Then, I realize that Jake is still in the room, staring intently at us, and that Nacio just kissed me to mark his territory. Although, right now, I'm happy he did.

Nacio gets a handle on the situation long before I do. He says, "If you need anything else, just leave a message with her assistant."

He takes my hand and pulls me out of my office before Jake or I can protest. I let him lead me out of my office as people stare at us with smiles on their faces, obviously happy to have a new suspect to add to their growing list of guys I might be dating.

Once we get outside, I expect to find his black Mercedes. Instead, I see George standing outside of his car with a smile, like he was expecting me. He holds the door open until I climb in, followed by Nacio. The door shuts, and before I even realize it, George has begun driving.

Nacio still has ahold of my hand, and I feel his thumb rub over the ring that I'm not sure if Jake or he was the one who bought it.

"This one is my favorite. I thought this would be the one you chose to wear," he says, smiling.

I sigh. "You are the one who bought the jewelry for me?"

He stares at me for a moment. "You think Jake got you the jewelry?" He raises an eyebrow at me.

"No...I just wasn't sure. Well, Jake said..."

He shakes his head. "There is no way that scumbag is capable of picking out anything half as nice as this."

I glance back down at my ring as Nacio is still holding my hand.

"He did get you something though." He begins rummaging in his pocket. He pulls out a skinny rectangular box and hands it to me.

I curiously look at him. "Did you forget to give me one of the pieces of jewelry?"

Nacio shakes his head. "No. This is from Jake."

"And how did you get it?" I say as my eyes widen.

"Jake left it for you this morning, but I didn't want you to confuse it with the gifts I got you."

I slowly open the box, curious as to what Jake bought me. I see a tiny bracelet covered in jewels. I can tell from looking at them that they are fake diamonds and rubies, not like the jewelry Nacio got me. This bracelet probably cost no more than a hundred dollars, while Nacio easily spent thousands, possibly totaling a million. And I know a million to him isn't much money.

But I can see now why Jake was pleased with himself. The red from the bracelet matches the color of the ring that Nacio gave me. Jake must've thought that he had done well in picking it out since it matched a ring he thought I'd bought for myself. He didn't realize that Nacio had given me that ring only today.

I glance over at Nacio, who's looking at the ring. He's clearly not happy that Jake also decided to get me jewelry on the same day that he decided to.

The car suddenly comes to a stop, and I glance around, looking for the restaurant that Nacio might be taking me to. But I don't see any restaurants. All I see are condo and apartment buildings.

"Where are you taking me?"

"I'm not taking you anywhere. This is my apartment building. I asked George if he wouldn't mind dropping me off here before he took you to wherever you wanted to go."

He leans over and softly kisses me on the cheek, gentler than he's ever been before. I watch him climb out of the car without so much as a good-bye, and then he begins walking toward what I assume is his apartment building, leaving me behind in the car.

I stare down at the bracelet that Jake got me. A bracelet that does nothing to make me want him back. And, while jewelry and materialistic things aren't what makes me want to be with Nacio, it does show me that he's willing to at least try. Try to do something nice for me to show me that he cares.

And, right now, I don't care about my damn promise to myself to stay away from Nacio. Right now, all I care about is getting the date he promised.

I toss the cheap bracelet onto the seat next to me and then holler to George, "I'll be right back."

I can practically feel George smiling at me in approval. He wouldn't have gone along with Nacio's plan, or any man's plan, if he didn't approve of them in the first place. I climb out of the car and run after Nacio, getting to him just as he begins walking inside.

"Wait!" I reach out and grab his shoulder.

Nacio stops and slowly turns around to face me. I can see the hope slowly filling his eyes as he looks at me, slowly erasing the tiny drops of fear that I saw there.

"What about our date?" I ask.

He sucks in a breath. "What about it?"

"Why aren't you taking me on a date, like you promised?"

"Because you told me that we couldn't do this, that we couldn't be together, and I'm trying to respect that while still protecting you."

"I don't buy it. What were all those gifts for all week if you weren't trying to win me back?"

"I guess I was hoping that I could still win you back. And, if not, then you could at least find some pleasure in the gifts every night, knowing that somebody loved you... even if"—he glances down at my stomach and then back at me—"the father doesn't. I just want you to know that I love you and that you aren't alone, not that you need any help."

When I don't say anything, he continues, "Even if you don't still love me, I'll always be here."

I glance up at him. "I still love you."

"I know."

"So, how about that date? I'm starving."

I watch as his grin slowly appears on his face.

"Sure."

"Just as friends though. You have to promise me that we won't end up back here at your apartment at the end of the night. Promise?"

He flashes me his sexy grin, and his eyes change from fear to lust. "Promise."

8

SCARLETT

My alarm sounds on my phone, and I roll over. I barely open my eyes, just far enough so that I can find my phone on the nightstand next to my bed. I hit the alarm off. I rub my eyes, still feeling exhausted. My alarm goes off every Saturday at seven, no matter what I did the night before. No matter if I was out drinking or partying or simply just working late. I know I'd feel worse if I slept in.

My body feels tired, but I slowly climb out of bed. I am immediately hit with queasiness in my stomach. Since I got pregnant, it's hit me every morning and often throughout the day. I know I need to quickly head to the kitchen to make myself some toast and eggs before the queasiness becomes too much. Usually, just getting a little bit of bland food in my stomach is enough to settle it.

I rub my eyes again, trying to force myself to wake up. I wake up enough to begin walking to my kitchen, but I stop in my tracks when I see a large flat screen TV on the wall across from my bed, which is odd since I don't have a TV in my room. I glance back at my bed, except it isn't my bed. Instead, a large black bed sits in the place where my white bed frame is supposed to be. A man is sleeping in the bed where no man should be.

I'm not at my apartment. I'm in Nacio's.

I don't have time to think about how I got here. All I have time to deal with is getting food into my stomach and fast. I sneak out of Nacio's bedroom, careful not to wake him. It takes me too long to find his kitchen. This apartment is massive, and it makes me wonder if he's living here with someone else because there is far too much space in this apartment for just him. I don't have time to think about that now though.

Instead, I search for food. Any food, anything, to make the nausea go away. I throw open the pantry and find it completely empty. Not one thing sits inside. Not crackers or junk food, not even stale bread. I try the fridge next and come up almost just as empty. I only find a couple of beers and a bottle of ketchup. I start opening the rest of the cabinets in the kitchen, hoping that maybe he stores some food in one of the other cabinets.

But, after searching almost all of them, I come up empty. I don't find any food. I hardly find any other items in the cabinets other than a couple of plates and glasses but no pots or pans or cooking utensils really of any kind.

I move to open the last cabinet when I feel my stomach decide that enough is enough. I glance around the kitchen for a trash can but don't see one. It must be one of those pullout-type cabinets. Despite opening most of the cabinets, I haven't seen the trash can though.

So, instead, I run to the sink just as I begin vomiting. I hate the feeling. As a kid, I would do everything possible not to get sick. I hate being sick, and I'm a terrible patient to take care of. I always think I know how to take care of myself better than anyone else. When I think my stomach is finally finished, I turn on the faucet and rinse out my mouth in the sink.

"Are you sick?" Nacio asks, standing at the entrance to the kitchen.

I wipe my mouth with a paper towel I found next to the sink. I shake my head. "Just need to get something in my stomach."

"There's a little café that has breakfast around the corner. I can go pick something up for you. I don't want to leave you alone though if you're sick. I can call Santino and have him pick us up something, or I can see if they deliver, but I don't think they do."

I shake my head. "I'm not sick. Just give me a second to get dressed and brush my teeth, and I can go with you. I'm not sick, just pregnant," I blurt out without thinking.

Realization at what I let happen last night slowly takes over my mind again. I destroyed everything I'd been working so hard to protect these last few months. One stupid mistake last night has ruined everything. And, in doing so, I've put everyone's lives at risk—Kinsley's, my baby's, Nacio's, and my own life.

In an instant, I remember. My memories come flooding back.

I remember going to a nice steak house with Nacio. I remember talking about nothing, yet talking about nothing was everything because we didn't talk about all the shit we were dealing with. We didn't talk about what Nacio did for a living or his family or my job or my family. We didn't even talk about my baby or who the father was.

Instead, we talked about our favorite music, movies, food. Instead, we told silly stories from our childhoods. Instead, we talked about things that people typically considered unimportant but always were important.

ELLA MILES

And, last night, I learned that we had virtually nothing in common.

I had been brought up as a beauty, and he had been brought up as a beast.

I like all things beautiful and pretty. I like making the world a better place. I have hope in the good of the world.

Nacio had been brought up to be a killer, to destroy the world, to see only the bad in people.

And those upbringings affected everything, including what food, music, and movies we liked. The experiences in our pasts affected our futures.

Still, it was an enjoyable night. I loved having a normal conversation with him even if we had nothing in common. Somehow, that made everything that much more exciting.

After dinner, I climbed into the back of the car with him, and George began driving us toward Nacio's apartment to drop him off. I remember every second that passed by as I sat next to Nacio in the back of that car. I remember wanting nothing more than for him to rip off the dress I was wearing and to take me right there on the backseat even though George could see us.

But Nacio did nothing. He stayed silent and honored my earlier request not to let me come up to his apartment. To just stay friends and be nothing more.

So, when George pulled up at Nacio's apartment, I said, "I need to pee. Mind if I use your bathroom?"

Nacio opens the door to his apartment and flicks on the lights while I stand behind him at the entryway.

This has to be one of the nicest apartments in New York

City. It's the penthouse, and it has large, expansive windows, just like my apartment does. The only difference is that these are at least twice the size as mine with a much more spectacular view of downtown.

"The bathroom is down the hall, to the left," Nacio says, breaking me from my spell.

I nod and make my way toward the bathroom. I get inside and close the door even though I don't need to use the bathroom. I just used the restroom at the restaurant before we left. But I guess being a pregnant woman and having to pee every five minutes sometimes has its advantages. Really, it was just an excuse to come up to his apartment.

I spend my time in the bathroom, trying to decide if I should really risk everything.

Is he really worth it?

Yes, he's worth it.

I don't know if it's how horny I've been these last few months without a man to keep me satisfied or the fact that my vibrator simply isn't cutting it anymore or if my pregnancy hormones are finally catching up to me, but I'm desperate for him.

All through dinner, I could barely concentrate because all I could think about was how I needed his hands on me. I needed his mouth pulling and tugging and kissing on my lips. I needed him buried inside me, making me scream. I needed him.

And, now, no matter how much my brain is telling me not to because, in the morning, I will realize how much of a mistake this is, I have to.

I flush the toilet and wash my hands in the sink. Then, I open the door to the bathroom and slowly find my way back to the living room where Nacio has made himself comfortable on his dark leather couch with a couple of fingers of scotch that he's sipping slowly.

I walk over and take a seat next to him on the couch. "You have a nice apartment. Does anyone else live here with you?" I ask, wondering if Santino or Reina live here at least part-time. Or if he uses it as an apartment for his employees when they have work to do here in New York. Or if there is a girl living here with him.

"No. I live here by myself."

I let out a breath I didn't know I had been holding.

"I just recently bought this apartment when I realized I'd be spending a lot more time in New York."

I don't know why it makes me feel relieved to know that no one else lives here with him, not even family. But it obviously would have bothered me. And, as for the part about him spending a lot more time in New York, I know the reason—me.

"Can I get you anything to drink? Some wine maybe? Or I think I have some gin somewhere, or you can have some scotch if you're up for it?" he asks, and then he frowns when he realizes his mistake. "I'm sorry. I wasn't thinking."

"It's okay." I don't want him to think about my pregnancy. I don't want him to hesitate to fuck me.

I begin slowly sliding on the couch toward him, my black dress inching up higher and higher as I do.

Nacio raises his eyebrows at me but doesn't say anything. Instead, he takes another sip of his scotch. I inch closer again, and my dress goes up even higher, now barely covering my underwear. I watch his eyes stay glued on my bare legs. And I'm happy that I wore this curve-hugging dress, despite wishing I had worn sweatpants into work today. I'm not showing yet, but I feel plenty bloated enough to already want to trade in my dress for something more comfortable.

I slide a little closer and watch Nacio squirm a little as he takes another sip of his scotch, trying to be good. Trying not to give in to his desires.

"I think you should go home now. I can call George and tell him you're ready for him to take you."

"You're not going to take me home?"

"No. I don't think that's a good idea."

He takes another sip of his scotch even though there isn't much left at this point. He's trying to avoid my gaze and my body, but the scotch isn't going to help him for much longer. My hand finds its way onto his chest and then moves up his body to his neck. I grab the nape of his neck and pull him toward me until his lips are hovering over mine.

"Kiss me," I whisper over his lips.

He doesn't hesitate to ask me if I'm sure that's what I want. His lips just devour mine, not allowing me to hesitate either or think or do anything but kiss him back. He takes all my air, my thoughts, with the kiss.

He pushes me back, moving quickly to keep both of us from thinking this through. He pushes me until I'm flat on my back on the couch, our mouths locked together. And, despite how much I know we shouldn't be doing this, it's the best feeling in the whole world.

His kisses demand more and more with each one. His hand tangles in my hair, and I feel his erection pressing against my stomach. I know I have only seconds left to stop this, to say no, before we both get so lost in each other that we won't be able to stop.

I don't want to say no though. Instead, I say yes.

I grab the hem of his shirt, and I begin tugging upward, needing to see his chiseled hard body above me, on me.

Needing this to go further than a junior high make-out session on my parents' living room couch.

He doesn't get the hint though because he keeps kissing and devouring me, not letting our lips leave one another, and I slowly let myself get lost back in his kisses. I forget about everything, even what I want, except to kiss this man whom I'm madly in love with. But, with each kiss, I come closer and closer to destroying his life.

Beast finally comes up for air, and as he does, he pulls his shirt off over his head. "God, I missed this."

I bite my lip. "Me, too." I grab the hair on the base of his neck and pull him back to me, not able to go another second without his lips on mine.

I've never felt this way before. I've never needed a man in my life as much as I do right now. Before, I only needed sex, which is what I could get with any one-night stand. But, now, I need so much more, and he's the one I want more with. Right now, what I need is lots and lots of sex.

Nacio finally gets on the same page as me when my moans turn desperate beneath his lips. His weight shifts off me just slightly, and his hands disappear underneath my dress. I feel my panties being pulled down my body, replaced with his skilled fingers. His fingers move slowly around me, teasing me, taunting me, but never giving me what I really want. But I'm not a patient woman, and I don't plan on waiting a second longer to get what I want.

I bite his bottom lip and firmly put it into my mouth to grab his attention. "I want you now. I can't wait, Beast."

I release his lip and lap at his wound with my tongue. Then, I grab his hand and help him push his fingers inside me, showing him that I'm not willing to wait. I scream out from how good it feels to have him touching me there again after so long.

His eyes watch me come undone with just his fingers. "You have to be patient, Beauty."

"I can't," I moan as he expertly slides in and out of me, making me moan, crazy with need.

My panting grows so hard that I can barely breathe, let alone talk or command him to do what I want him to do. I want him to take me, but he's taking his sweet time. I begin to try to focus on my breathing, to slow it down so that I can tell him what I need between kisses, while his fingers glide back and forth inside me. But, every time I get close, his fingers take me further away, and I'm close to losing my mind instead of growing closer to him being inside me.

This time, when his fingers slide back out, his cock slides in, and I finally get what I really want. Somehow, in the midst of everything, I close my eyes and push everything out, but when I do, all my feelings come rushing in.

"Open your eyes, baby."

I do. I look at him even though I know it's a mistake. His eyes have so much love that I could cry. And then I do. I cry as he fucks me. I cry as he slides in and out, and for some stupid reason, every time he moves, I cry harder. I've never been a huge crier to begin with. I cry during the normal times, like at sad movies, the loss of someone, or after a tiring day. But I've never cried in the middle of sex.

Right now, I don't care what Nacio's thinking as he watches me cry. Instead, I just enjoy it. He doesn't move fast. Instead, we find our own slow rhythm together as I figure out what I need from him—love.

We move together in unison until I come with him buried inside me, and he comes just after with our eyes locked together. He doesn't collapse on top of me like he usually does after he comes.

Instead, he looks deep into my eyes and says, "I love you,

Beauty, and don't ever forget that." He wipes the tears from my cheeks before kissing away the remaining ones on each cheek.

I lie on the couch, exhausted, and watch as Nacio stands next to me before lifting me into his arms.

"Where are we going?" I ask tiredly, practically falling asleep in his arms.

"I want you in my bed."

I yawn and stretch my arms over my head, but the second our bodies hit that bed, I know I'll be ready for round two. But we both know after a good night's sleep comes clarity, and that clarity will remind me that we can't be together.

And just like I thought last night, the clarity sets in this morning. But with the clarity comes confusion because I'm just as torn as I was before. "I need to go."

Nacio runs over to me as I begin searching for my things around his apartment. I spot my purse slung over the arm of his couch in the living room, and I make my way over there.

Nacio stops me though, grabbing ahold of my shoulders and forcing me to look up at him. "You're not going anywhere until I get you some breakfast and make sure that you're okay."

"I'm fine. I need to go home." I brush past him and am able to snatch up my purse before he gets to me again.

"Please, just let me take care of you. It doesn't mean that we have to start dating again or be together in any real capacity. Just let me take care of you. Please."

I look down at what I'm wearing—his T-shirt and

shorts. It'll have to do because there's no way I'm squeezing back into the dress that I wore over here. I just need to get George to take me home, and then all I have to do is walk into my apartment. I don't care what I'm wearing for that.

"I need to go now. I need to get some things sorted out in my head. I'll call you later." This time, it's my turn to reach up and kiss him on the cheek and then walk away without a good-bye.

I walk out the door of his apartment, and I'm gone before he has a chance to come after me.

9

SCARLETT

I SPENT the entire weekend on my couch in my apartment. Thinking. Trying to come up with any way possible that what I just did last night with Nacio didn't just ruin everything I'd worked so hard to protect. At the same time, I was also trying to find a way to get Nacio to fuck me again and again and again. Because, after Friday night, I know now more than ever what it means to give up Nacio. And it's not how I want to live the rest of my life. I want to live my life experiencing that over and over and over again.

By the time I get to work on Monday morning, I'm even more clueless than I was before. Preston is sitting at my desk, waiting for me, as I get into work. I'm a little disappointed when I notice that no gifts are covering my desk like usual.

Preston notices my disappointment and says, "He left you a note."

I watch him hold up the note in his hand. I reach out to take it, but he pulls it back out of my reach.

"So, where have you been all weekend?" he asks.

"I've been at home, alone, lying on my couch and watching Netflix."

"Sure you have. You haven't been sucking face with Mr. Nacio Marlow, have you?"

I walk around to the back of my desk and snatch the note out of his hand. "No, I haven't."

Preston gets up from my chair, and I take a seat as I begin opening the note from Nacio.

"Then, why does the note say that he's sorry if he fucked up the other night but that it was one of the best nights of his life, and if you let him, he'll repeat it every night forever and ever?"

In frustration, I hit Preston's arm with the note. "You read my note? Don't you know that's an invasion of my privacy?"

"Not according to you. I'm one of your best friends. You share everything with me, remember?"

I roll my eyes but don't argue with him any further. "What's on my schedule for today?" I ask.

Preston looks at me, and I know he has something really important to tell me, but he doesn't want to tell me.

"What is it?" I ask, getting frustrated.

I see the determination in Preston's eyes as he prepares to tell me whatever he has to say.

"You need to start telling people about the baby, Scarlett. You can't keep waiting."

"He already knows about the baby," I say, exacerbated.

"The whole truth?" he says, raising his eyebrows at me.

"Enough."

Preston shakes his head. "You have to tell him everything. You need to talk to Kinsley, too."

"I'll tell them all everything when I'm ready. I'm not ready yet."

"And why not?"

"For lots of reasons that I don't have to explain to you."

With every second that passes, I get more and more frustrated with this conversation. Preston walks over to me.

I stand because I can tell from the look on his face that he needs a hug, and honestly, so do I. I know he's just pressuring me because he is looking out for me. We hug.

I don't know how everything got so messed up. But it did. I used to have a simple life. The only thing I worried about was what was going on with the company, but lately, I haven't so much as thought about what's going on with the company. It's been the last thing on my mind.

When he steps back, he asks, "Have you told Kinsley about Nacio?"

"Has she told me about what with Nacio?" Kinsley asks as she stands in the doorway to my office.

I look at Preston, and he's giving me an I'm-sorry-but-not-really-that-sorry look on his face. I turn from Preston to Kinsley. "Just that I'm less worried about him coming after us again. It's been a long time since it happened, and I just don't want to live in fear every day."

Preston motions to me that he's going to go, and I nod. Then, I'm left alone in my office with Kinsley.

"So, what are you doing here today? Not that I mind you stopping by anytime. I just have a lot of work to catch up on today. You'll have to ask Preston if I can do lunch or something later."

Kinsley narrows her eyes at me, not concerned at all with my words. "Now that he's gone, are you still going to lie to me?" she asks.

"Am I going to lie to you about what?"

"Don't play dumb with me, Scarlett Bell. You know

exactly what you're lying to me about. I want you to tell me the truth right now!"

My eyes widen as I look at my best friend who thinks I've deceived her in some way. I have, but I just don't know in which way she's talking about. Although she shouldn't be this mad at me if she understood why I lied to her and deceived her. Every time I deceived her, it was to protect her, to keep her safe. But I haven't seen Kinsley this mad at me in a long time, not since I stole her Barbie doll and cut off all her hair before giving it back to her in the second grade.

But I'm not going to start admitting to things until she tells me what she's upset about. I've protected her for too long to stop doing it now.

"I don't know what you're so upset about. Just tell me. I'm sure I have a reasonable explanation for it."

Kinsley crosses her arms over her chest as her eyes bulge, big and wide. "I saw you with him."

"Who?" I ask, still playing dumb. But I know who she's talking about.

On Friday night, I was afraid, when Nacio took me to the restaurant near where Kinsley and Killian live, that we were taking a chance in getting caught. But that was half of the fun and excitement of it. And I didn't actually think we would get caught.

I plead with God, *Please, God, no, no, no, no, no, this can't be happening. I couldn't have ruined everything in one moment.*

Except it is happening.

"Nacio."

I nod. Not sure of what else to say.

"How? Why? How is this possible?"

"I…" I open and close my mouth, trying to figure out what I can say to help her understand. But I don't think anything I say will help.

If I can't explain my relationship with Nacio to my best friend, how in the world will I ever have a chance at explaining it to the world?

But I have to try.

"I fell in love with him before I even knew who he was. And, now, I'm not sure I can let him go. Kins, I've tried letting him go. I thought it was the only way to protect him and you. But I've failed."

I watch as the fear in her eyes turns to anger.

Her face tightens, and her cheeks flush bright red as her eyes narrow on me. "I just don't understand. How could you not know who he was?"

"I don't know. I just didn't."

"How could you?" Kinsley asks as her voice trembles. "After all the horrible things he did. After what he did to me. He's killed who knows how many people. You're just okay with that?"

I guide her over to the couch, afraid she is going to pass out if she doesn't sit down.

I don't know how to look her in the face when I answer. I know I need to tell her the truth, but the only way to help her understand would be to lie. That option isn't great, so I go with the truth. "Yes, I'm okay with it."

Kinsley runs her hand through her blonde hair and then stands from the couch, unable to even sit next to me. "You're okay with the fact that he's a smuggler? That he trafficked women and children? That he killed them when they didn't behave? That he is a killer?"

My tears sting my eyes. Today, I am going to have to give up someone I love. Either Kinsley or Nacio. They can't coexist together.

"Yes."

"You're okay that he tried to kill me twice? You still love him, even after that?"

"But he didn't try to kill you. He saved you."

Kinsley glares at me with her gorgeous eyes that have turned cold. "He didn't try to kill me? Are you fucking kidding me? So, I just saw bullets flying past my head twice, but neither of those times, he was trying to kill me? He was trying to protect me?"

I nod even though I realize that now is not the time to argue the point with her. I can't even really prove that he was saving her those times. I just know it to be true. She's already decided that Nacio is a monster, and right now, there's no point in trying to convince her otherwise.

She sits back down on the couch, and I take her hands in mine.

I plead, "I wish I didn't love him. Everyone's lives would be easier if I didn't. If I hadn't fallen for him. But I did, and now, I can't take it back. I can't make it go away, no matter how hard I wish I could."

Kinsley's eyes soften a little but not enough.

I know she can't understand, but I try to make her understand anyway.

"When you first met Killian, was he the guy you thought he was? Was he the perfect man with no flaws?"

"Don't you dare. Don't you dare compare Killian to Nacio. They're not even in the same stratosphere."

I try a new approach. "What if Killian had been a killer? What if he had killed dozens of people? Would you still love him? If you'd already fallen in love before you found out, would you still have married him?"

"That's not fair. Killian isn't a killer. Nacio is. I would've never been so stupid to fall in love with a man who was a monster."

Her words hurt more than she knows. Because I was stupid enough to fall in love with Beast. And I'm not certain that a beauty can turn him back into a man.

I take a deep breath to keep the tears from falling. I don't want her to see me cry, to see how badly she's hurt me. "Maybe I am stupid for falling for him. But there's nothing I can do about it now."

Kinsley raises her eyebrows at me. "There's plenty you can do now. For me, you can stop seeing him and turn him into the police."

"I can't."

"Sure you can. I'll go with you. You just go to the police and tell them you didn't realize who he was, and as soon as you found out, you turned him in. It's that simple."

"I can't."

"Why not?"

"Because I love him."

"What about me? What about my feelings? Do you even care about me?"

"Of course I do, Kins. I just love him, too, and it's not as simple as just giving him up."

Kinsley stares at me in disbelief. "Fine. If you won't, I will."

She turns to leave, but I run to the door, blocking her exit.

"Please, Kins, you don't have to do this. We can figure something else out. Please just give me a little bit more time to figure it out."

"I can't," Kinsley says.

I move away from the door and watch as my best friend walks through it, leaving me all alone and ending our friendship that I'm not sure can ever be healed again.

10

BEAST

SCARLETT'S GONE. Again.

I got her back, and I lost her, all in a stretch of a few hours.

I'd never expected to get her back so soon. I hadn't thought that, once I got her back, I'd ever lose her again.

But, now that I have, it sucks even worse than before.

I hear a knock at the door, and I can't help but let a little bit of hope back in at the thought that it could be her. Or it could be about a million other people. I try not to get my hopes up, but it's too late. If Scarlett isn't standing on the other side of my door, I'm going to be devastated.

I run to my door, hoping to God that Scarlett is standing on the other side, but as I get closer, I can feel it in my gut that it's not her. She just left this morning. There is no way she would come back so soon. She wanted time to think, to figure out if she still wanted to be with me.

Unlike her, I don't need time. I already know we are supposed to be together. I just don't think we will ever end up together. I don't think I deserve a happily ever after. I don't deserve her.

I reach for the doorknob and turn it before throwing the door open. Santino is standing in the doorway with a smug look on his face.

"What do you want, asshole?" I ask, walking back to my kitchen to pour myself a scotch. I know it's too early to start drinking, but I need the alcohol if I'm going to survive today without her.

I pull a glass out of the cabinet and then pour myself a glass. Santino reaches into the cabinet and pulls out another glass. I frown but pour some of the scotch into his glass as well. Maybe I won't have to deal with much of his crap if he's drunk.

He takes a drink as he stares at me, studying me, like he will be able to tell what I'm thinking just by looking at me. He probably can. It's clear to see that I'm not thinking about anything other than Scarlett.

I walk from my kitchen to the living room, collapsing on the couch where I fucked Scarlett just last night. A couch that I should replace if I want any chance at keeping my sanity. Not that I could ever part with anything that Scarlett touched.

I watch as Santino takes a seat on the love seat, kitty-corner to me. His eyes are still studying me.

"Reina send you?"

He nods.

I frown and take another sip of my drink.

I always thought that Santino would be on my side. I thought he would always be loyal to me, but I'm not so sure anymore if he's loyal to me or Reina. Or maybe he thinks he can be loyal to both of us. He can't. Not anymore. He has to choose, just like we all do.

"What does she want?"

"For me to convince you to kill them."

My eyes widen. "Them?"

His eyes fill with sadness. "Yes. Kinsley and...Scarlett."

I stand as I throw my drink down on the ground. I watch the glass shatter, and the liquid covers my hardwood floor. I never thought that Reina would stoop so low as to have a woman I loved killed. I thought we were closer than that.

Now, I realize what she really wants—to control me.

"That's not going to fucking happen."

"I know. I told her as much."

"Then, why are you here?" I ask, staring him down. I have to know if he is on my side or hers.

"To let you know, so you can protect them and keep them safe."

I growl. I don't know if I believe him or not. Right now, my concern though is keeping Scarlett and Kinsley safe. Keeping them alive. If something happens to either of them, I'll die.

I pace the room, trying to figure out a plan on how to keep them safe. My mind is racing though, so it makes it hard to think straight. To think of any sort of plan.

"Talk to me. Let me help you. I want to protect them, just like you. There is no way we are going to let Reina do this."

I turn and glare at him. Then, I let my anger and fear get the best of me. I rip him up from where he is sitting and shove his body against a wall. My arm holds him, pinning him against the wall.

But, unlike all the other times when I've pulled something like this on him, he doesn't fight me. He just lets me hold him against the wall, like he deserves it. I ease off just a little, confused by his behavior.

"I want the same thing that you do," he says calmly.

"I can't trust you."

He narrows his eyes. "You don't have a choice."

I let him go and walk away because he's wrong. I always have a choice. And my choice is not to trust anyone right now.

I hear a knock at the door, and I stop and look back at Santino, who is still standing against the wall.

"Who is that?" I ask.

He shrugs and then walks back to where his scotch is sitting next to the couch. He picks it up without looking at me.

I sigh and then make my way toward the door. I swear, if it is Reina or someone else she sent to convince me to kill Scarlett, I'll kill them right now. I reach for my gun in the back of my jeans as my other hand goes to the door. I glance back at Santino to see what he is doing, but he seems unfazed by whoever is at the door.

I turn my attention back to the door, ready to shoot if I need to, and then I open the door.

"Scarlett?" I ask, like I'm not sure it's really her standing in front of my doorway.

She glances down at the gun in my hand, hardly seeming fazed that I'm pointing a gun at her.

"I'm sorry," I say nervously before I holster my gun in the back of my jeans.

She shakes her head as she walks into my apartment, like she's at home. I wish this were her home. I wish we could move in together, like any other normal couple.

"Don't be sorry. You should be ready to protect yourself," she says.

SHE WALKS into the living room and drops her purse on the

floor while I curiously look at her, wondering why she is okay with me pulling a gun on her.

She notices my stare and continues, "Kinsley knows."

I cock my head, not understanding what Kinsley knows. "You told her about your pregnancy? About who the father is?"

She shakes her head. "No. She saw us together."

I smile. "Okay."

She runs her hand through her long brown locks with curls that have come loose, hanging down past her shoulders. "Okay? That's all you have to say? You're in danger."

I smile and reach up to tuck her strands of hair behind her ear. I get lost in the smell of her hair as I touch her. I'm just so happy that she's here, that I can touch her again. Hold her, be with her.

"Nacio," she says sternly, trying to break me from my dream.

I glance back at her, trying to focus. "Yes?"

"You aren't taking me seriously. This is serious. Your life is in danger. You could end up back in jail, or Killian could hunt you down and kill you before the police have a chance to take you to prison. I can't...that can't happen."

I smile and touch her cheek, trying to calm her. It works. She closes her eyes and just feels my hand pressed against her cheek. When she opens her eyes, I see tears.

"I can't lose you," she says in a whisper.

"You won't."

I move my hand to her chin and lift her mouth up to meet mine in a gentle kiss. She purrs a little in her throat as I kiss her. And my cock takes it as an invitation. I ignore it, knowing now isn't the time or place, even as much as I want it to be. I need her desperately, and I think she needs me, too. To show her that I'm still hers and that no one is going to take me away from her. But, first, I have to talk to calm her nerves.

"You don't need to worry about losing me. All you need to worry about is keeping yourself and your baby healthy. Let me worry about the rest."

She stares at me, and then she notices Santino sitting on the couch, watching us. She smiles for the first time since she stepped foot inside my apartment.

"I missed you, Santino," she says, walking over to him.

He stands, and they hug. "I missed you, too."

I glare at Santino as his hands tighten around Scarlett. He meets my glare but doesn't taunt me with the fact that he is touching her and I'm not. I don't see jealousy in his eyes. In fact, I think I see...

I shake my head. Santino doesn't care about anyone but himself. He's loyal to his family. That's it. He doesn't care about her.

Scarlett pulls away. "He's not going to listen to me, is he? He's not going to protect himself?" she asks Santino.

Santino looks from her to me. I stand frozen with my hands in my pockets.

Santino turns back to Scarlett. "No."

Her face drops.

Santino lifts her chin. I want to attack him again until he says, "Don't worry though, Beauty. That's why I'm here. To protect him and you. I'll make sure nothing happens to him even if he won't listen to you."

Santino looks at me, and it's the first time I start to believe him. Not enough to trust him to protect Scarlett yet, but I do believe he cares about her.

He gently kisses Scarlett on the cheek. "I'm glad you're back, Beauty. He's been a mess without you," Santino says. He turns and begins walking down the hallway. "I'll see myself to one of your dozens of bedrooms."

I smile and watch Santino leave before I walk over to Scarlett. "Listen to him. You don't have to worry about me."

She shakes her head. "That's all I do. Worry. About you, the baby, Kinsley. I'm not going to just stop now."

I touch her cheek again, needing to touch and comfort her, to stop her from worrying about something that is not worth worrying about. "You don't need to worry about me going to jail. They don't have anything on me, and as far as Killian is concerned, I can take care of myself."

"What do you mean, you don't have to worry about going back to jail? They have you on camera, attempting to kill Kinsley." She pauses for a second, thinking. "How did you get out of prison in the first place?"

"Don't worry. I got out legally, despite what Killian or the media might have reported. I got out for good behavior. I was on probation for a while. I'm not anymore. And they don't have me on camera. I'm a pro, remember? I made sure that the security cameras didn't record anything that night."

"But they have Kinsley's testimony. Her word is a lot more believable than yours."

I sigh. "Maybe so, but it would never get that far."

"Why? What do you know?"

"Just trust me. I'm not in any danger." I don't add that Kinsley and she are the real ones in danger. I don't want to cause her any anxiety that could affect the baby. I'll only tell her if she needs to know to stay safe, and right now, she doesn't need to know.

"I'm sorry," she says, twisting her hair in her hand.

"You have nothing to be sorry for."

"I do. I should have made sure that Kinsley never found out. I know that I've sent you mixed signals about what I want when it comes to us, but I can't lose you. You can't go back to prison."

I take her hands in mine, loving the feeling of her smooth skin. "What if I deserve to go to jail? What if everyone will be better with me gone?"

"I won't be better. I need you."

She might as well be promising me forever because that's how I take her words.

"Promise me, you'll do everything you can to keep yourself safe?" she asks.

"Only if you promise to do the same."

I can see the hesitation in her eyes. She doesn't want to promise. She thinks she needs to protect me. That my life or Kinsley's might be more important than her own.

I raise my eyebrows at her, waiting for a response that I never get. Instead, her lips claim mine. This kiss is mind-numbing. And I feel her promise with her lips, signifying that she will do whatever she can to protect herself.

Because she is mine. Forever.

And, this time, after I'm done with her, I'm not letting her go. No matter what excuse she gives me.

I need to show her that she is mine.

My hands run over her body and lift her as she wraps her legs around me. I fist her mane of hair, holding her tight to my body, as I kiss her everywhere that I can get my lips. On her lips, her neck, her chest. I'm desperate to have her, to claim her, like I really want. I should have done this the first time I saw her. I should have claimed that she was mine. I was stupid to ever let her think that she was anything but mine.

I carry her to my bed, not believing that she just left my bed this morning. I thought she was gone again, and I never imagined I would have her back in it so soon, but if I have my way, she won't be leaving my bed for the rest of the week.

I lay her down on my bed and kiss her soft lips before I stand up.

She whimpers when I stop kissing her. "Please, I need you."

I kiss her, and her whimpers stop.

"Don't worry, Beauty. I'll give you everything you need and more."

I grab the hem of her shirt and lift it over her head before removing my own shirt. I remove my jeans and briefs, needing to feel her skin against mine as soon as possible. She watches me as I do, studying my every movement. I undress her until she is completely naked, and then I climb on top of her, kissing my way down her body.

"This is mine," I say as I kiss her neck.

She moans her agreement.

"And these, these are mine," I growl as I kiss each of her breasts.

I continue kissing until I get to her still perfectly smooth stomach. A stomach that contains a baby, despite not showing any outward signs to indicate her secret. I know it's there. Taunting me that she slept with another man so quickly after she left me. Right now, she's not all mine. She's still his, whoever he is.

I kiss her stomach, over every inch. "And this..."

She grabs my hair, trying to pull me back to her lips so that she can silence me.

I don't let her. I kiss over her stomach again. "I don't care whose sperm created the baby." I slowly and deliberately kiss her stomach as I keep my eyes locked on hers. "This is mine."

She sucks in a breath as I lower my kisses until I'm

kissing her pussy. She jumps from the unexpected touch, and then she moans as my tongue swirls around her folds.

"This is mine."

"I'm yours," she says, looking at me.

I lower my mouth to her pussy again, making sure she's good and wet, before I take her the way I want. And then I claim her again and again in every way.

"You're mine, Beauty." I insert a finger into her pussy. "Mine."

She bites her lip to keep from screaming.

I place another finger at her ass. I slowly insert it, filling all of her. "Mine."

She bites her lip harder to keep from moaning louder.

I remove my fingers and then place my cock at her entrance. I forgot to grab a condom, and I begin to reach down to grab my pants off the floor to search for the condom that I know is in the pocket, but Scarlett stops me.

"You don't need a condom."

My eyes widen.

She trusts me, and I trust her.

I've never fucked a woman without a condom.

I slide into her, and the feeling is different. I can feel all of her against me. Every drop of her liquid covering me. The tightness of her pussy. I can feel it all.

My lips move to hers as I rock slowly in and out of her, getting used to the new feeling of her. She keeps my lips on hers, trying to muffle her screams.

"Moan for me, Beauty. Let it all out."

She shakes her head. "Your brother is in the next room," she whispers.

I laugh. "I don't care about him. You're mine, and I need you to tell the whole world that you're mine."

I thrust again, making sure to rub against her clit, as I

kiss her neck. She moans but still tries to stifle it by digging her mouth into my shoulder.

I'm not going to let her keep quiet. I need the whole apartment building—no, the whole world to know that she's taken.

I lower my lips to her nipple and nip at it while I thrust, driving her wild. I hold her hands over her head to keep her from using them to cover her mouth, her screams. She tries biting her lip again to keep herself from screaming, but I bite down as I pull an orgasm from her.

"Nacio!" she screams.

I growl as I shoot my cum inside her. And then I collapse, holding on to her, needing to feel that she is mine.

"You're mine, Beauty."

"Forever," she whispers back.

I hold on to her tighter as our breathing gets slower, deeper, and I know that we will soon let sleep take over us. I'll have to wait to claim her again until after we've both slept. I just hope, when we do, clarity won't change how she feels again. That she will understand that she's mine.

11

SCARLETT

I STIR out of my zombie-like sleep. I don't know how long I was out, but it was long enough to dream of what my life could be if everything were different. If Nacio and I could just move in together and do normal couple things, like going to dinner, watching movies, and sleeping in. How I long for the simple things like that in our relationship instead of worrying if he's going to end up in jail or dead.

I slide out of bed, careful not to wake Nacio. As much as I wish that we had a life where we didn't have to worry about someone killing us or ripping us apart, that is exactly what I have to worry about. I get dressed and sneak out of Nacio's bedroom.

I need to go see Killian. I need to find out what the police or FBI is planning. I need to know how to keep Nacio safe because he clearly has no concern for his own safety. I grab my purse and then leave Nacio's apartment without waking him.

I don't call my driver, George. I don't want to let Nacio or anyone else know where I'm going. I need to talk to Killian without worrying if Nacio is going to try to find me and get himself thrown in jail.

I flag down a cab, and once I climb in, I give the driver Killian's work address. I try not to think as the driver pulls into traffic, but all I can do is think.

I touch my stomach as I think about what Nacio did. How he kissed my stomach. How he called the baby his even though he knows full well it isn't.

It made me fall more in love with him. It also made me that much more desperate to save him.

I wanted to tell him who the father is, so he could understand that the baby would never be his.

And, because of this baby, I could never be his. Not really.

Because I have to choose between him and this baby, and as much as I love him, it's not even a decision. I have to choose this baby.

A tear drops, and I wipe it away. I just wish it were that easy to wipe Nacio away. I wish I had never met him. I was just fine with being alone.

The cab driver pulls up in front of Killian's work. I pay him and climb out without a word. I don't see anyone as I walk into the hotel where Killian works. Not because they aren't there, but because I can't see them since I'm too focused on finding Killian.

"Scarlett?" Killian asks as he pauses in front of me, finding me before I found him.

"Hey, Kill. Can we talk?"

He reluctantly nods and then pulls out his cell phone. He types something in before he looks back at me. "I can spare a few minutes. Come on, let's go to my office."

"Thanks."

Killian walks me to his office and then takes a seat

behind his desk while he motions for me to take a seat opposite him. I do, dropping my purse to the floor, feeling strange about sitting on this side of a desk. It makes me feel less in control.

"Why are you here, Scarlett?" Killian asks as he stares at me with anger in his eyes.

"How is she?"

He stares at me, trying to read me. "Kinsley doesn't want to speak to you right now."

"And you?"

He narrows his eyes. "I'm talking to you because she can't."

I suck in a breath, trying to keep from crying again. I lost Kinsley, I'm going to have to give Nacio up, and I'm going to lose...

I can't even think about it.

"I'm sorry," I whisper.

Killian looks away for a moment and then back to me. "She hasn't gone to the police yet. She's torn up about what to do."

I nod.

"I haven't gone to the police yet either," he says.

"Thank you."

"Don't thank me," he says, angrily getting up from his chair.

I watch as it slides backward and slams against the wall.

"I haven't told them because of her. I don't want to go against her wishes. But I'm not going to let her get killed. I'm not going to let that man anywhere near her ever again. We've increased security." He pauses and then looks at me with tears in his eyes. "Do the right thing, Scarlett. Turn him in. End this."

"I can't do that," I whisper.

"She needs you, Scar. She needs you."

I get up from my chair and hug him because that's what we both need.

I slowly let go. "Just give me some time to figure this out. He won't hurt Kinsley. I promise you that."

He sighs. "I'm going to the police with this first thing next week if you don't."

"Thank you."

He shakes his head, and I know I've disappointed him.

I walk back to where I dropped my purse on the floor, and I dig through it until I find the envelope that I've been carrying around for a while now. Kinsley needs to see it. I hold out the envelope to Killian.

He curiously looks at it but takes it. "What's this?"

"It's for Kinsley."

He narrows his eyes at it.

"Just have her open it with you when you see her next. It doesn't have anything to do with Nacio."

He stares at it as he holds it in his hand. "I don't think she is going to want to read any notes from you. She's really not in a good place right now, Scar."

I swallow hard. "I know, and I'm sorry. But she needs to see what's in the envelope. Just promise me that you will make sure she opens it."

He nods.

I hate that he doesn't promise, but I didn't promise him that I would turn Nacio in.

There's nothing left to do. The envelope is my only hope at restoring my relationship with Kinsley. Now, I just have to figure out how to protect Nacio.

12

BEAST

I STARE DOWN at my phone as Scarlett walks out of the hotel where Killian works. I pull out my wallet and throw some bills down to pay for the coffee I ordered while I waited for Scarlett to get done talking to Killian.

I get up and follow her at a safe distance. I want to see what she is going to do. *Is she going to go to the police?*

I don't care if she does. I just want her safe.

I followed her here shortly after she left my apartment. When I'd woken up, she was just gone. But I'd put a GPS tracker on her phone the first time I was with her. I won't let her out of my sight, especially not now that Reina wants her dead.

I should kill Reina for threatening to take Scarlett's life. I should, but I can't. I can't kill Reina any more than I can kill Scarlett or Santino. She's family.

And I understand why she wants me to kill Scarlett, too. To protect herself and her family. In Reina's mind, Scarlett knows too much to stay alive. If she's not with us, then she's against us. And anyone against us must die, so we can protect ourselves.

I watch as Scarlett climbs into another cab instead of having George drive her. I shake my head. She thinks I can't track her if she isn't with George. She doesn't understand that nothing will stop me from tracking her. From being with her.

I climb into my car that is parked down the street and follow her cab. Her cab turns toward her apartment, and I sigh because I know I can protect her at her apartment. I've set up enough cameras and alarms to ensure that I can watch her and keep her safe.

I park at the end of her block and watch her walk inside her apartment. I pull out my phone and pull up the cameras that are hooked up in her apartment just in time to see Scarlett entering her apartment.

She looks tired and worn down as she drops her purse the second she gets inside her apartment. She walks to her fridge and pulls out some Chinese takeout. Then, she begins eating from the box without bothering to heat it up.

As much as I want to, I resist the urge to pick up some real food for her and run it up to her apartment. She doesn't want to be with me right now. I won't go up unless she isn't safe. And, although I could make a good argument for cold Chinese food not being safe, I don't think she would see it that way.

She carries the box of food with her as she goes upstairs to her bedroom and then to her bathroom. She turns the faucet to her bathtub on, and she begins to undress. I've watched her many times on the security cameras, but I never watch her undress. I never invade her privacy like this. But I can't keep my eyes off of her as she undresses.

I watch her slowly remove her shirt, and I can see the lace of her bra hugging the top of her breasts. She cracks her neck from side to side, trying to get the tension to leave her body. Then, she slips out of her pants until she is standing in just her underwear.

My cock twitches as I remember the feeling of taking her without a condom, of claiming her. I want to do it again right now. I growl instead, forcing those thoughts from my head.

When I look back at the screen, she's completely undressed and climbing into the tub. She stretches before she lies down in the tub. She grabs the carton of Chinese food and begins eating again. She takes a while to finish eating and then places the carton on the edge of the tub. She leans her head back and closes her eyes, trying to relax, but I can see her tension, even from here.

I want her to relax. I need her to relax.

I pull her number up on my phone and dial before putting it on speakerphone so that I can still watch the security cameras. I watch her look to the floor when her phone buzzes. She sighs as she reaches down to grab her jeans and pull out her phone.

"Hello?"

"Hi, Beauty. I miss you. I wish you hadn't run out on me."

She smiles, happy to hear my voice. "I miss you, too. Sorry I ran out on you earlier. I just had some errands to run, and I didn't want to wake you."

"You sound tired. Can I come take care of you and help you feel better?" I ask seductively.

She smiles. "I wish you could. I have a couple of more errands to run, and then I can stop by."

I frown. I don't want her to go anywhere else. I want her to stay with me where it's safe. I also want her to feel better. To relax after whatever that fucker Killian told her.

"That's too bad. I was just about to take a bath, and I was

hoping your naked ass could join me. I wanted you wrapped around my cock while the jets and my hands massaged you."

She sighs, and I can see my words affecting her as she adjusts herself in the tub. Her cheeks flush from her just thinking about it.

"God, that sounds nice."

"It's not too late to join me."

She bites her lip. "It's too late. I'm already in my tub at my apartment."

I growl into the phone. "It's not too late."

I hear a tiny gasp.

"I can still please you from here."

I watch as her hand goes to her chest, and I know her heart is beating quickly.

"How?"

"By getting you off with just my voice."

I hear her swallow hard on the other end of the phone.

I grin. *This is going to be fun.* "Lay your head back on the back of the tub."

I watch on the screen, but she doesn't do it.

"Is your head lying back yet?"

"Yes."

"You're lying. Trust me. Lay your head back against the side of the tub."

She glances around the room, wondering if I'm there, but then she does as I said.

"I am."

"Good girl. Now, I want you to touch your finger against your gorgeous lips and suck it like it's my cock. Get it nice and wet for me. Imagine it's my cock."

She does exactly as I said, and my cock hardens. I reach

my hand down, needing the release, but I stop. This isn't about me. This is about her.

So, instead, I watch her suck her finger.

"Now, I want you to rub your nipple, swirl your finger around it."

She does, and from just watching her, I think I might come in my pants like a teenager, not an experienced man who has been with too many girls.

"How does it feel when you touch yourself?"

She purrs. "So good. God, I wish you were here, touching me."

"Close your eyes. I'm there. I'm touching your nipples, squeezing them hard."

She does exactly as I said, and I watch her chest rise and fall as she does.

"I'm lowering my hand from your breast, over your smooth stomach, and between your legs."

I watch her do just as I said.

"I'm rubbing your pussy in slow, torturous circles."

Her hand slips between her legs under the water, but I know what she is doing—rubbing herself.

"Yes, Nacio," she moans.

"I find your clit as I slip a finger inside."

"Yes."

"And then I fuck you with my fingers."

She does just that. "Fuck, Nacio, I'm going to..."

"Come for me, Beauty."

I watch her explode on the screen, not feeling anything but bliss.

A rap on the window makes me jump out of my seat. I glance over and see Santino climbing into the passenger seat next to me.

"What the fuck are you doing?" I ask.

"Scaring the shit out of you." He glances at the phone that I have been holding in my lap, and then he smiles. "Did I interrupt something?"

"Yes! Now, get the hell out!" I turn the phone away, so he can't see Scarlett. "I said, get out!"

"Reina is tired of waiting. She put out a hit on them."

"Both of them?"

He nods.

"Fuck."

I jump out of the car and begin running toward Scarlett's apartment building. There is no telling how long Reina has had the hit out or which one of her killers has been assigned to the job. My security cameras won't do anything to protect Scarlett. I need to protect her. Now.

I burst through the door of her apartment building with Santino on my heels. He's just as concerned as I am. And, to protect Scarlett, I also have to protect Kinsley.

"Go get Kinsley!"

Santino freezes. "Where do you want me to take her?"

"I'll let you know."

I keep running and then stop again. I shout back to Santino, who has already begun running in the opposite direction, back out of the building, "And don't kill anyone!"

He freezes and smirks.

"Well, don't kill anyone that Scarlett would hate us for killing."

"Don't worry, Nacio; I'm not the killer in the family."

I run toward the elevator, not even registering what Santino said. I just keep running. I get to the elevator, and over and over, I press the button to go up, waiting, as the elevator takes its sweet-ass time getting down to the ground floor. A man steps out, and I shove him as I climb in, needing him to get out faster so that I can make it up to Scarlett.

I press the button for her floor and then the button for the doors to close, begging them to close faster so that I can make it upstairs faster. They finally close, but then I'm stuck in this cage, unable to move or do anything to protect her. I'm helpless.

The fear sinks in that, in these few moments I'm not with Scarlett, Reina could have her killed. Scarlett could be dead. I pull the gun from the waistband of my jeans. If she is, I'll kill everyone who even so much as thought about killing her.

The doors open, and I rush out, not stopping until I reach her door. I don't bother knocking. Instead, I pull the key that I have to her apartment and unlock the door with my gun drawn. I step inside, looking for any signs that anyone has broken in, for any signs that anyone is here to kill her.

I keep moving, quickly scanning her apartment, until I get to her bathroom. I throw the door open without thinking, just needing to know that she is okay.

She screams, still in the tub, and she starts scrambling, trying to grab a towel, her phone, or anything that might protect her.

"Shh...it's okay. Scarlett, it's just me. I'm not going to hurt you."

She wraps the towel around her body. Then, she finally sighs. "Then, why are you aiming a gun at me?"

I realize that I still have my gun out, pointed right at her. I lower it but don't put it away. I haven't checked every room in her apartment. She might not be safe.

"What are you doing here?" Her face turns red. "I thought you were at your apartment? That's at least a twenty-minute drive, a lot longer in traffic. We weren't even on the phone for five minutes. How did you get here so fast?"

I swallow. "I've been sitting outside your apartment the whole time."

She tightens her grip on the towel around her. "What were you doing?"

"Protecting you."

She glances around the room and then spots something in the corner. She runs over to it, looking up, staring at the tiny camera. "You've been watching me! Haven't you?"

"Scarlett, this really isn't the time. I need to get you out of here. You're not safe here."

She stares at me with wide eyes, frozen. "You've been watching me!"

"Scarlett, stop. I need you to come with me. Now. I'll tell you anything you want later."

"I'm not going anywhere with you. I thought you were done with lying to me. I guess I was wrong."

I don't have time to deal with her, to explain. I need her safe, and I need her safe now.

I walk over to her and scoop her up. Then, I begin carrying her out of her bathroom while she begins hitting me, trying to get me to let her go.

"Let me go."

"No."

I feel her towel slipping off her body, but I'm not letting her go. Not for a second.

I begin walking toward the front door of her apartment.

"Where are we going?"

"Somewhere safe."

Her eyes grow wide as she studies me. "What's going on?"

"I don't have time to explain. We just have to get out of here now."

She grabs my chin to force my eyes to look at her, and I pause for a second, letting her know how serious I am.

"I will carry you out with nothing but a towel on, Beauty. I have to protect you."

She takes a deep breath. "Just let me put something on."

I study her eyes, afraid it's a trick. If I put her down, she might make a run for it.

"Trust me," she says.

I slowly lower her to the ground. "Fine, but I'm not letting you out of my sight, and it has to be quick. We can get you new clothes later."

She nods and runs back upstairs to her bedroom. I follow with my gun in my hand, scanning to make sure that no one is going to touch her.

She moves to her closet and pulls out some sweatpants and a T-shirt. I don't think I've seen her in anything this casual before, but she looks just as beautiful as always.

She freezes as she ties the sweatpants so that they will stay up around her waist. "What about Kinsley? Is she in danger?"

"Santino is making sure she's safe."

"I need my phone. I need to call her. I need to warn her and Killian."

I shake my head and grab her arm. "We don't have time. We have to go now. Santino is on it. He will protect her."

"I have to call her—"

"Think about your baby, Scarlett. You have to protect your baby. Kinsley will be fine. Trust me."

She hesitates for just a second longer, and then she takes my hand. "Okay."

13

SCARLETT

I TRUST NACIO. I do. More than I even think he realizes. If I didn't trust him, there would be no way I would go with him after I found out that he'd put cameras all over my apartment. He says they are for my protection, but then why would he need to put a camera in my bathroom? I trust him though. So, instead of refusing to leave with him, I'm riding in the passenger seat next to Nacio as we drive to who knows where.

I glance over at Nacio, who is focused. More focused than I have ever seen him. I have questions. So many questions. But I don't ask any of them. I trust him to keep me safe, just like he trusted me to keep him safe. He shouldn't have. I can't keep him safe any more than he can keep me safe.

I close my eyes as the images of the men I helped kill flash in front of my face. Neither of us deserves to be safe. We both deserve to die for killing.

The only one who doesn't is this baby, I think as I touch my stomach. *This baby is innocent. This baby deserves to live.*

"Where are we running to?"

"Somewhere safe."

I sigh. Nacio is terrible at communicating with me, at being honest with me.

"Whom are we running from?"

Nacio briefly closes his eyes and then opens them, and I see the pain.

Reina.

We are running from his sister. And it's killing him that he is protecting me from someone he used to spend all his time protecting.

I want to ask if Kinsley is okay, if Santino found her safe and sound. I wonder what he is doing to protect her. Is Santino dragging Kinsley out of her home right now, forcing her into a car, and driving her here? Because I know that Kinsley won't go willingly if that is their plan.

Nacio doesn't know anything about Kinsley though. His phone hasn't rung once since I've been with him. He knows nothing more than I do, so there is no point in asking. There is no point in worrying. I can't do anything to protect her right now. I just have to hope that Santino got to her in time. I trust him almost as much as I trust Nacio. Santino will do everything he can to keep her safe.

"How long have the cameras been in my apartment?" I ask instead.

"Since the first time I fucked you."

"So, you have been watching me on the little cameras. Watching personal things. Watching me undress and bathe and, and, and...pee."

His lips curl up into a tiny smile, and it makes me smile.

"You're worried that I watched you pee? What kind of a creep do you think I am?"

We smile at each other.

"I never watched you get naked or pee or do anything

like that. I put the cameras up strictly as a way to protect you. The only time I ever watched you while you were naked was today."

I shouldn't believe him. I mean, what man wouldn't watch a woman he was attracted to while she was naked on a video any chance he got? But, for some stupid reason, I do.

"Okay, I believe you. But you still haven't said you're sorry yet." I raise my eyebrows at him.

"That's because I'm not sorry."

"You're not sorry? How can you not be sorry? You invaded my privacy. You stalked me."

He smiles. "I'm. Not. Sorry. Everything I did was to protect you. You would have never allowed me to put those cameras up if I had asked permission and told you that your life was in danger. That, just by being involved with me, your life would always be at risk. Always be in danger. I have to protect you from that, and that means not telling you everything."

"No."

His eyes widen as he glances from the road to me. "I will protect you without worrying you. You don't deserve to live your life in fear because of me."

"No. If I'm going to be with you, we'll do this together."

"No," he growls.

I ball my hands into fists to keep from strangling him. "Nacio, this is never going to work," I say, trying to keep my voice calm. "We are in this together. I have to be a partner. We can't—"

"Get down!" Nacio screams at me.

"What?" I cock my head at him, not understanding what he's talking about.

"Scarlett, get down!" Nacio pushes my head down between my legs.

"Nacio, what—"

Nacio swerves the car as a pop and crack make me jump. I try to peek up to figure out what the unfamiliar sound was, but Nacio pushes my head back down.

"I swear to God, Scarlett, if you don't stay down, I'll—" He never finishes that sentence. Instead, he swerves again as the loud popping comes at us, this time louder and longer than the first.

Gunshots.

Someone is firing at us, I finally realize, as a bullet hits my window.

I scream, expecting the glass to break, but somehow, it doesn't. Instead, when I glance back up, there is a spot where the glass is cracked, but it didn't shatter on top of me. I don't know how that's possible, but I don't ask. There are more important things to worry about, like figuring how we can both stay alive.

I turn my head to Nacio, who has sped up and is now holding a gun in one hand with the other on the steering wheel.

"Who's after us?"

"Reina's men."

Nacio glances in the rearview mirror and then speeds up as he swerves the car. I grab ahold of my legs, the only thing I can hold on to, as he makes a hard right. I can feel my stomach rumbling, telling me it's not happy with the car ride. It needs to empty itself, but I push that away. I can't vomit. It would distract Nacio, and what he needs right now is to focus to keep us both safe.

He swerves the car again and then stops suddenly before speeding up again. The movement almost does it. I feel liquid sloshing in my stomach, but I don't vomit.

"Is there anything I can do?"

"No, just stay down, Scarlett."

Nacio doesn't even glance my way as he drives. I hear more shots firing at us, breaking glass.

I scream again and keep my eyes on Nacio, praying that he doesn't get hit. He doesn't. The glass next to his head has cracked but hasn't broken. The car is bulletproof, I realize. I don't know much about how bulletproof cars work, but I do know that we aren't completely safe. A bullet can still get through; it's just harder.

I don't know what to do as more shots ring in my ears. I feel completely helpless. My heart is racing as I hope that we all stay alive—Nacio, the baby, and me.

We have to stay alive.

I don't know how many people are chasing us. I don't know how many cars surround us. But, when I look at Nacio, I see a calmness that shouldn't be there. He's been in this situation before. This is where he thrives.

I, on the other hand, feel useless. I can't help him as much as I want to. I can't save him or protect him. I'm helpless.

The only thing I can do is try to keep myself alive. So, that's what I do. I stay bent over while Nacio protects us.

He drives faster and faster, and I'm afraid we are going to crash. I don't know how he is going to get us out of this situation. But I know that he will. I have faith that he will save us, and in his eyes, I can see that he believes he will, too. There is no other option.

"Stay down, and brace yourself," Nacio says.

I do.

And, for a split second, he glances at me out of the corner of his eye. It's just long enough for us to see the love in each other's eyes, and that could be the last thing we take with us if we die. It's a moment that I will take with me forever, and it'll probably be the last thing that goes through my head before I die, no matter if it's in the next few seconds or years from now.

And then his eyes aren't on me anymore, but my eyes are on him.

He stomps on the brakes.

My heart and world stop.

The car spins deliberately.

The window on his side goes down, leaving him vulnerable but allowing him to aim the gun out of the window.

He gets off a shot, and I hear loud popping sounds that make me want to squeeze my eyes shut to shut out the world and pretend this isn't happening.

I don't though. My eyes stay on Nacio. I watch him squeeze the trigger again.

But the car keeps spinning faster and faster until my vision goes blurry.

I can't see anything.

I can't see Nacio.

I can't feel my heart beating.

I can't tell if I'm breathing.

I can't tell if either of us is even alive.

I feel the car move again, so I must be. We must be.

We begin moving faster again, and the sound of bullets hitting the car becomes fainter and fainter.

I feel my heart beat. Once. Twice.

Then, it beats quickly, so fast that I can no longer keep track.

I breathe again, and the fog begins to clear.

Nacio.

He's still alive. He's driving the car fast but nowhere near as fast as we were going before.

I touch my stomach, and I know the baby is still alive.

I'm still alive.

I don't have to ask Nacio if I can sit back up. I know it's safe.

The threat is gone. For now.

I feel it in the air around us.

I slowly sit up, wincing a little as I do.

"Easy," Nacio says, putting his hand on the back of my head as I ease up. "Easy. I think you hit your head on the dash."

I feel my forehead, and I don't feel any blood, but it's sore, so I must have hit it against something even though I don't remember it.

"How do you feel?" he asks.

"A bit dizzy."

He holds the back of my neck, rubbing harder than what feels nice, but I don't dare tell him to stop rubbing. I need him to touch me, reassuring me that we are both alive.

I take a couple of deep breaths as the fog and dizziness continue to clear out of my head.

I look at Nacio clearly for the first time. "Are you okay?" I ask.

"Yes. You're alive."

I smile and lean into his hand that is now on my cheek. I close my eyes and then open them again.

I don't ask if we are safe. I already know that we aren't. There is just no immediate threat right now.

I reach out to touch his face, but we hit a bump, and my hand lands on his arm. He winces when I touch him.

My hand automatically jerks back, and then I see why he winced, as blood stains my hand. I see blood trickling out of his bicep. It doesn't look like that much blood, considering a bullet is in his arm.

"We need to get you to a hospital."

"No."

My eyes widen, but this time, I'm not taking no for an answer. "Damn it, Nacio! You are going to a hospital even if I have to call an ambulance to chase us all over the state. You can't protect me if you're dead."

He smiles. "Glad you have finally realized that I am the one who needs to worry about protecting you."

I frown. "This isn't funny, Nacio. You could die from this."

He laughs. "I'm not going to die. I was hit by one bullet. I'm barely bleeding. It just hurts like a motherfucker."

I lean over toward him and take a closer look at his injury. It doesn't look too bad, but I'm not a doctor. I know nothing about injuries like this. For all I know, he could die from this.

"It could get infected."

"It won't."

"You could bleed out."

"Unlikely."

"You could—"

Nacio traps my lips with his, shutting me up. He kisses me like a man who is very much alive, not like a man who is in danger of dying.

"Where are we going then? You can't just leave the bullet in your arm. You need medical treatment."

"We are going somewhere that Reina thinks I would never go—to one of our childhood homes in the Hamptons." He grins. "And, as far as medical treatment goes, I think it's your turn to save me."

14

BEAST

I TURN onto the street of the house where I spent so many summers. A house I vowed I would never go back to. And never, ever voluntarily. Yet here I am, driving toward the monstrous house, the only one on this street. I glance out my window to the grass that belongs to my family, despite still being a couple of miles away.

I try to keep my focus on Scarlett and why I'm doing this —to keep her safe. But it kills me.

The second that I said where we were going, Scarlett understood what it meant. How hard it would be for me to drive here after what happened here. After I hurt my sister here and, in turn, destroyed myself.

I glance over at Scarlett, and she is staring out the window at the water flowing by next to us because, of course, our house has one of the best views in the Hamptons.

It's worth it though to know that she is alive. That she will be safe here.

I will never forget the terror I felt when I saw them pull up behind us. I'd been in similar situations before. I'd felt the adrenaline that comes with being in that situation, but I never felt the fear. I'd never cared if I lived or died. I still don't.

But, the second I saw the cars behind us, I wasn't sure if I could save her. I wasn't sure I was strong enough. I had no idea what to do. I just reacted.

I don't know how we got out of there alive. We're lucky that all that happened was a bullet to my arm. It should have been so much worse.

They had three cars. We had one.

They had guns, too many guns. I had one.

The only difference was, for the first time in my life, I had something to live for. Someone to save.

I'd never driven so fast once I realized that she had to live.

I'd never had my mind be so focused.

I'd never known exactly what to do before I even did it.

I'd never shot so perfectly.

I'd never been so thankful in all my life.

I drive to the end of the street where our house stands proudly on the hill. A house we should have bulldozed a long time ago. Instead, it's still here. My father's dead, long gone. He was the only person who gave a shit if this house was still here. The second he died, Reina and I should have destroyed the house. Instead, we chose to never think about it again, but it was always there, in the backs of our minds, just like the memories that always haunt us.

I park the car and take a deep breath as I look at the overgrown yard filled with weeds. It's been a long time since anyone came here to take care of the house. But the house still stands proudly behind the weeds, taunting me.

Scarlett takes my hand and gently rubs it. "Come on, let's go inside. The sooner we go inside, the sooner you will find out that I have no idea how to fix your arm, and the sooner we will get out of here and go to a hospital, like I wanted you to."

I chuckle. She does that to me when I need it the most.

I nod and then let go of her hand so that I can get out of the car. I walk to the back and pop the trunk to retrieve my bag that is always there with extra guns, ammo, and medical equipment for situations just like this.

I walk around to Scarlett's door that she tried to open but can't, from the looks of it. I try the handle, but it doesn't budge. I pull on it again, using my whole body, and I feel the pain in my shoulder. When I finally get the door open, I hold my hand out to her to help her out. She takes it, staring at the cracked glass. If it wasn't bulletproof, one or both of us would have died.

I pull her to me and kiss her, as much for me as for her. We both need something to wipe away what happened and to remind us that we are alive.

The kiss is perfect, but it can't take away the pain in my arm. It just helps her to understand the pain as well, and she pulls away. I try to pull her to me, but the pain is too much.

I've been shot before, and I know what's coming next. The adrenaline is leaving my body, and with it gone comes the pain that I barely felt before.

She takes my hand again. "Come on, let's get you inside."

With the bag in one hand and Scarlett's hand in the other, I walk us to the door of the house. I drop the bag and grab the handle, praying that it's unlocked because I don't have the strength or energy to deal with breaking in. It turns, and I push the door open before picking the bag back up and leading Scarlett into the house.

We step inside, and Scarlett coughs as we both breathe in the layers of dust covering the house. It's clear that no one has been here in years. I walk over to the light switch, flipping it up without thinking, but no lights come on. There isn't any electricity, just like there won't be any air-conditioning or water. Maybe this wasn't my smartest idea.

I guide Scarlett into the kitchen. I don't have to think or guess where to go. I just walk automatically, as if I were here yesterday. I stop when I get to the faucet, flipping it on but no water comes out.

We will have to make a run for supplies later. Right now, I have to deal with my shoulder.

I walk over to the kitchen table, drop my bag on top, and then pull two chairs out. I motion for Scarlett to take a seat in one. She does, and I take a seat in the other, trying not to move my right arm that is now all I can think about.

With my left hand, I pull my bag to me and start to unzip it with the help of Scarlett, who holds the bag while I pull the zipper. I begin digging around in the bag to find everything that we are going to need. I find the painkillers and antibiotics. I pop the bottles open and take some of each without water. Scarlett watches me as I do.

I reach back into the bag and pull out the medical bag that contains the rest of the things Scarlett is going to need. With a terrified look on her face, Scarlett watches me as I pull each item out of the bag.

"You can do this," I say, trying to reassure her.

She gives me a tight smile, but I can tell she doesn't believe me.

I take the water bottle and hand it to her. She takes it, curiously looking at me.

I lift the sleeve of my shirt up so that she can easily see the wound.

"I need you to flush out the wound with the water."

She nods and slowly begins moving toward my arm. I know, if she can't even do this step, this is going to be a long process. She unscrews the top and then holds my arm with one hand as the other slowly moves closer with the water bottle. Her scared eyes focus on the wound, like the bullet is going to jump out and attack her, too.

"You need to flush out the wound with the water. Understand?"

She nods and then begins to flush my wound with the water. It burns, but I don't move.

She swallows hard when blood along with the water pours down my arm.

"That's good," I say.

She stops, and I see her chest slowly rise and fall. Despite being scared to death, she's calm. She can do this.

"I need you to look at the wound. There is a bullet in there, correct?"

She looks up at me and then puts her hands back on my arm as she moves in closer to study my wound. "I think so. Yes, there is a bullet."

"Okay, if you think you can do it easily, you need to try to remove the bullet without injuring anything."

She nods.

"Good."

I begin arranging all the items she will need on the table.

"You need to slowly open all the instruments, careful not to touch them. Then, put on the sterile gloves, and pick up the tweezers."

She takes a deep breath but begins doing as I said. When she has the gloves on with the tweezers in her hand, she freezes.

I grab her chin and force her to look at me. "You can do this, Scarlett. Use the tweezers and pull the bullet out of my arm."

"It's going to hurt. I can't hurt you."

"It's going to hurt worse if you don't remove it."

She nods.

"Good girl."

She takes ahold of my arm with one hand, and then with her other hand, she begins to insert the sterile tweezers. I bite down, trying to keep from making a sound or moving, as she digs into my wound.

Fuck, it hurts.

I growl through my clenched teeth.

She doesn't look at me when I growl. She ignores me and stays focused on her task at hand.

I bite down, trying to keep from yelling or cursing, as she digs the tool deeper into my arm, but I can't keep from cursing.

"Fuck, that hurts. Hurry." I clench my teeth again as I feel her pulling the bullet out.

When the bullet is out, she applies pressure with the gauze, and I can finally breathe again. As she watches the blood soaking the gauze, I can't take my eyes off of her. I'm in awe of how strong she is.

She applies new gauze, tightly holding it to my arm that still hurts.

"I think the bleeding has slowed enough. Now what?"

"Clean the wound with some water again."

She does so as I contemplate how she should close the wound. It's too big to heal on its own or with medical tape. It will have to be closed with either stitches or staples. I decide on staples since it will be faster.

When she's done cleaning it out, she looks at me with

big eyes because she knows what she needs to do next but not how. She's worried, but pulling the bullet out was the hard and risky part. This part will be easy, and then all we have to worry about is infection. The antibiotics should help with that. And Santino is good in a medical crisis. He will be able to help once he gets here.

I pick up another pack of sterile gloves and put one on my left hand. I pick up one of the sterile tweezers.

"Pick up the other tweezers and the staple gun."

She does so, holding one item in each hand. This would be easier with two people and four hands, but we don't have that luxury, and I don't want to take the time to show her how to stitch up my arm.

I look down at my arm and grab ahold of one side of my wound with the tweezers. "Grab the other side until it is touching mine."

She takes a deep breath and then pulls the wound together with her tweezers. She pushes a staple into my arm without asking or telling me she's going to do it. The pain from the staple is nothing. I barely wince when she does it.

I move the tweezers over to the next stop, and she does the same. We repeat the process over and over until the wound is closed.

She drops the tweezers and staple gun onto the table and then takes off her gloves while I do the same.

We both stand at the same time, our hands grabbing each other's faces, and we lock our lips together.

We've survived.

We keep kissing, tangling our tongues together, our bodies together, as we cling on to the lives that we shouldn't still have.

We kiss anywhere we can get our lips. We take turns

kissing each other's lips, necks, ears, cheeks, chests. Anything that is visible, we lay our lips on it.

Scarlett needs more though. She drops to her knees and pulls at my pants, undoing the buckle and zipper and pulling down until she finds my cock. Her lips wrap around it, needing more and more.

When she touches me, I growl, feeling my fire finally returning to me. Finally truly feeling alive again since that moment in the car when I thought our lives were over.

She sucks and licks and pumps my dick like no woman ever has.

I fist her hair in my left hand as her eyes smile up at me. I want to fuck her when she's done, but first, I need to shoot cum down her throat. I need to—

Thoughts stop as the wicked woman takes me all the way into her throat.

She does it once, twice...

And then—

"Fuck, Scarlett," I growl as I tighten my grip on her hair and shoot my cum down her throat.

She smiles when I finish and takes her time with licking me until I'm clean.

She begins to tuck me back into my pants, but I'm not done with her. I reach down to lift her up to me.

She shakes her head. "I have something I need to tell you first."

"It can wait."

I begin pulling her up again.

"Really, Nacio? You couldn't wait until you found a bedroom?" Santino says, standing in the kitchen with an angry Kinsley next to him.

15

SCARLETT

I DON'T GET a chance to tell Nacio about what I need to tell him. I can't hide secrets from him anymore. It's burning inside me, and I need to tell him. But, just as I tried to tell him, Santino and Kinsley walked into the house.

I don't know how we didn't hear them earlier, but here they are.

I look at Kinsley standing next to Santino and notice his hand gripping her bicep. He forced her to come here. She didn't come willingly, like I had hoped.

"Kinsley," I say weakly, trying to smile at my best friend, who I know hates me right now.

I don't notice what Nacio or Santino are doing.

I walk toward Kinsley.

"You let him kidnap me!" Kinsley screams.

It makes me pause for a second. She's pissed, and she has every reason to be. But she is safe—or as safe as she can be—so she can be pissed all she wants, but I'm relieved. I should say I'm sorry, but I'm not, and I'm done lying to people I love.

"Let go of me," she says, trying to shake Santino off of her.

"Can't do that, sweetheart. You'll run," Santino says.

"Then, kill me already. That's why I'm here, right? You're going to kill us. Just fucking get it over with."

Kinsley jerks, trying to break out of Santino's grasp, but he holds on to her arm tighter.

"Kinsley, they aren't going to kill you or me. They are trying to protect us."

"You're wrong, Scarlett! They want to kill us. They've done this to me before. They haven't changed. They are going to kill us, and it's all your fault!" Kinsley screams, looking straight at me.

I take deep breaths in and out, trying to find a way to fix this. I will do whatever it takes to protect my best friend and keep her safe, including having Santino tie her up.

"Kinsley, they are protecting us. Their sister is the one after us, not them."

She shakes her head. "They don't have a sister."

I nod. "They do. Her name is Reina. I've met her. She's the one who sent men after us. They are protecting us from her men."

"No."

I see the tears in her eyes, and it kills me.

"We were shot at on the way here. We almost died. Nacio was shot." I point to him and his newly stapled arm, blood running down his side and onto the floor.

Kinsley shakes her head. "I don't believe you. If you were shot at, it's because he has too many enemies. Someone was just coming to seek revenge. That was all it was."

She's never going to trust me or believe me again until I

can show her that I'm worth trusting. And it has to have nothing to do with Nacio or Santino or this situation.

"Killian didn't give you the envelope, did he?"

"No, he didn't get the chance. This scumbag kidnapped me before he had the chance."

Killian.

Why isn't he here with Kinsley and Santino?

I don't know if he's safe or not. I need to ask Nacio about that soon but not in front of Kinsley and not until I'm sure that she trusts me again.

Only one thing will convince her to trust me again. To love me.

I walk slowly toward Kinsley as I watch more tears glisten in her eyes.

When I get to her, I glance to Santino. "Let her go."

To my surprise, he does without a fight. I pull Kinsley to me and hug her. She lets me but doesn't hug me back.

And then I whisper into her ear, telling her everything... things that I can't tell Nacio yet. I need him to protect me and the baby and Kinsley, and I'm not sure he will if he finds out the truth.

16

BEAST

"Do you think I would risk my baby if I didn't think they would protect us? No matter how I feel about him, no matter that I love him, I would never risk this baby," I hear Scarlett say.

She was quiet before, just whispering to Kinsley. But, now she's speaking so softly I can't make out what she is saying. My eyes stay on Scarlett; that's all my eyes ever do anymore. They consume Scarlett, everything about her. Every movement, every look on her face, every curve of her body, everything. I know it all.

"Fine," Kinsley says.

Her word gets my attention enough to look from Scarlett to Kinsley. I try to tell if she's lying or not, but despite my time with Kinsley, I don't have a clue about her. I haven't studied her face like I have with Scarlett. I don't know if Kinsley is telling the truth or just saying what we need to hear in order to trust her.

So, I look to Scarlett instead. She knows Kinsley. She knows if Kinsley is lying or telling the truth. And she believes Kinsley, so I have no choice but to do the same. I don't know exactly what Scarlett told Kinsley to convince her that I can be trusted, but I have a hunch it had something to do with Scarlett's baby.

Scarlett hugs Kinsley again. Both have tears in their eyes.

I walk over to them, needing to get this off my chest so that I can let them have the space they clearly need. "I'm sorry," I say to Kinsley.

She wipes her tears and lets go of Scarlett so that she can face me, strong and defiantly. "Sorry is not good enough. You shouldn't have taken me—again. The FBI could protect me from your sister. Killian could protect me." She pauses. "Killian. Is he okay? Does he know I'm okay?"

"The FBI couldn't protect you. Reina has people who have infiltrated the FBI. The FBI isn't safe. And, as far as Killian, he's safe. Reina doesn't give a shit about him. She doesn't kill unnecessarily. He's a smart man. He knows how to stay alive. The FBI will be able to protect him."

"Does Killian know where she is?" Scarlett asks.

"No."

I motion toward Santino to follow me out, so we can give them some privacy and figure out some sort of plan.

But Kinsley steps in front of me, stopping me. "Scarlett tells me you love her. Is that true?"

I glance over at Scarlett. "I love her."

"So, this is all to protect her from your sister? To protect me so that she doesn't have to suffer from the pain of losing me?"

"Yes, I'm doing this to protect her. I'm not a good man, you know that, but I love her. I'll do anything for her."

"Even kill your sister?"

My mouth drops a little at her question. "I don't think it will come to that."

I step around her to find Santino, but she pushes her way back in front of me.

"That's not good enough. If we are going to rely on you for protection, if I'm going to trust you, I need to know that you are putting us first. Will you kill Reina if you have to, to protect Scarlett?"

I take a deep breath in and out, trying to think about what I would do. Reina is my sister. I've protected her my whole life. She was the only woman I ever loved before Scarlett came into my life.

I see Santino standing behind Kinsley. He awkwardly shifts his weight, waiting for my answer.

If I killed Reina, it would destroy him and me.

If I let Reina hurt Scarlett, it would destroy Kinsley and me.

Neither option is a good one. That's why I will do everything in my power to avoid having to choose one or the other.

I turn and look over my shoulder to Scarlett. "I'll do anything it takes to protect Scarlett, including killing my sister if it comes to it."

Scarlett sucks in a breath as I promise to put her first.

I look back to Kinsley. "Satisfied?"

"For now," she says, frowning at me.

I've had enough of being questioned about where my loyalties lie. I brush past Kinsley and motion for Santino to follow me.

"Are you sure?" he asks, glancing back at the girls with obvious worry that they might run away.

I roll my eyes at his ridiculousness. "They are fine. Scarlett isn't going to go anywhere without me, and Kinsley won't go anywhere without Scarlett. We are all safe."

I keep walking, not waiting for Santino's response.

I walk back outside of the house where I can think. I can't think about anything in that damn house. I don't hear if Santino followed me out, but I assume he did, like the good younger brother that he is. I close my eyes and rub my forehead, trying to make the pain go away, as I think.

"There is no electricity. No running water. No food. I need you to go to the store and pick up everything we will need," I say.

"I can do that," Santino says from behind me.

I blow out air through my pursed lips, trying to push the pain out. "I'm going to need more painkillers, too. I'm almost out, and between my arm and head, no one is going to want to be around me if I'm in this much pain."

Santino chuckles. "No one is going to want to be around you either way."

I turn and look at Santino, and he stops chuckling.

"So, what's the plan since you are going to be all serious? Wouldn't this be one of the first places Reina looks?"

I glance at the house behind Santino. I can hear our father's voice telling me to be a man. To destroy my sister. I can hear my sister's screams. I can feel my own pain.

"No. This is the last place she would think that I would go."

Santino looks at me and then understands. "Are you going to be able to stay here?"

"Yes. I wasn't lying when I said I would do anything to protect Scarlett."

He nods. "So, what is the plan?"

"Right now, we stay here, and we wait Reina out and keep them safe."

17

SCARLETT

I STARE at my phone as the morning light peeks in through the windows. I didn't sleep, not one second. No one else did either.

I flick my phone on and off, staring at the clock that shows it's six thirty a.m. It's about the only thing I can do on my phone other than play a few offline games due to not having any reception here.

I roll over and look at Kinsley, who is picking at the threads on the blanket, pulling them apart and then braiding them back together. We are both lying on the floor in the living room, something we haven't done since we were kids. But we wanted to be together last night, and Nacio wouldn't leave us to a room on our own. Said it wasn't safe. That's how we all ended up sleeping in the living room, despite there being dozens of beds in this house.

I glance over at Santino, who is lying on one of the couches. He's snoring. He must have fallen asleep recently because, the last time I looked, he was awake, like the rest of us.

Nacio sits up on the couch next to me, watching us. But

he's not really watching us. He's reliving what happened to him here. I can see it in his eyes.

I chose to sleep next to Kinsley because I thought she was the one who needed me the most last night. Now, I'm not so sure.

Is this going to be my life from now on? Always having to choose between the two of them, never getting to choose them both?

Yes.

I get up off the floor because I'm not doing Kinsley any good by just lying next to her. Despite telling her about my pregnancy and doing my best to convince her that Nacio is a good man, she's still mad at me.

I don't blame her. I just don't know how to change anything. And I don't regret falling in love with Nacio.

I walk over to the couch and take a seat next to Nacio. "Stop thinking."

I pull his chin to mine, and I kiss him. He's hesitant at first, still letting his ghosts haunt him. He slowly, tentatively tries to let them go as he pushes his tongue into my mouth, but I can tell he's not really here. He's still being haunted. Still thinking, not really kissing me.

I grab the nape of his neck, digging my nails in harder than usual, trying to draw him to me. It doesn't work.

I try moaning as I kiss him, despite there being two other people in the room.

It doesn't work.

I try moving my hand over his cock over his shorts.

Nothing.

I pull away. "Nacio?"

"Huh?" he asks after a few seconds pass.

I frown. "Is there anything I can do to help you?"

"Just stay alive."

I nod my head. I don't know how long we are all going to last here in this house.

"I'm going to go make us some breakfast." I get up from the couch and head to the kitchen where Santino stored the supplies of food he brought back yesterday. I didn't see what he'd gotten, but hopefully, it's something good because I know Nacio isn't going to let me leave this house if we need anything.

I dig through the bags on the counter and find some protein bars, fruit, peanut butter, and bread. I sigh. I guess Santino could really only get nonperishable foods. I pull out a banana and a protein bar. I guess this will have to do. I hope we aren't going to be here long.

Kinsley walks up behind me. "What do we have for breakfast?"

I hold up the protein bar and banana.

"Yum, yum. Did he get any coffee?"

I shake my head. "Good thing, too. Just the smell of coffee has been making me sick lately."

She smiles. "Coffee used to give me morning sickness, too."

"You okay? I mean, I know this is tough, seeing me pregnant after..." I can't finish my sentence. I can't say, *after you lost Wesley*.

She nods. "This is a happy time, not sad. This is how it's supposed to be."

She reaches in and pulls out a bar and banana as well. "Do you think Mr. Safety would care if we ate our breakfast outside? I need some fresh air after breathing in all of this dust all night."

I bite my lip, knowing that Nacio isn't going to be happy about us being anyplace that isn't within his eyesight.

Kinsley rolls her eyes. "Hey, Nacio, Scar and I are going

to eat our breakfast outside. If you have a problem with it, get your ass outside to ward off whatever snipers are out there, waiting to shoot us."

I frown at Kinsley.

She huffs and then walks outside. I wait for Nacio to walk over to the kitchen.

"I'll give you some time alone. You should be just as safe in the backyard as in the house. The fence surrounding the property isn't climbable. I have an errand I need to run anyway," he says.

I frown. "Want some company?"

"No, Kinsley needs you more right now."

"What errand are you going on?" I ask, trying not to sound worried. But I'm afraid he's going to do something dangerous.

"It's nothing you need to worry about. Just going to get some security equipment, so I feel safer with us sleeping in actual bedrooms and moving about the house without having to stay right on top of each other. I'm afraid, if we stay in this house together for too long, we will be more of a threat to each other than Reina's men."

I smile, but it soon fades when I see something oozing from his wound.

"It's fine."

"It doesn't look fine. It looks infected."

"It's not infected. The oozing is good. The wound is cleaning itself out."

I frown. "It's infected."

He kisses me on the forehead, like I'm a child. "I'm taking my antibiotics. I'm fine. Don't worry about it."

I watch him dig through the bag and pull out a protein bar before he leaves. When he leaves my view, I walk out onto the deck where I find Kinsley lying on one of the couches, eating her protein bar.

I take a seat on a chair next to the couch and begin unwrapping my own protein bar.

"So, explain to me again why you're so in love with that monster?"

"He's good to me."

"You mean, good in bed."

I blush. "He's good in bed, but there is more to him. We just...connect."

Kinsley sits up and narrows her eyes at me. "And there is nothing I can do to change your mind? Nothing I can say about what I've been through with him to show you that you shouldn't be with him?"

I shake my head. "I've seen him at his worst, trust me."

"You've seen him torture and kill people?"

"Yes."

Kinsley leans back. "I always knew you were the wild one between the two of us. I just never expected you would fall for a criminal."

"It wasn't like I planned it. I just don't see him as a criminal."

"That's because he's never pointed a gun at your head."

I swallow, trying to avoid her gaze.

"He's pointed a gun at your head before?"

I bite my lip, trying to figure out how to paint Nacio in a better light for Kinsley instead of bringing up worse things about him. "Not exactly. We've just done some exciting sexual things," I say with a grin on my face.

Kinsley blushes. "I really don't think I can handle hearing about your sexcapades."

"Why not? I have had to hear about your boring married sex acts for the last ten years."

She frowns. "I miss him."

I get up off my chair and sit next to her on the couch. "I know, but he's safe, and you're safe."

"I just wish I could text him or talk to him and let him know that everything is okay."

I nod. I hate that we don't have cell phone reception here. "I'll talk to Nacio when he gets back and tell him we need to do that ASAP."

"You think he would really be okay with me doing that?"

I smile. "He will be if that's what I tell him we are doing."

She chuckles. "Glad you have him under your spell at least."

We each work on eating our protein bars for a while as we enjoy the nice morning weather outside. It's been a long time since I've had nothing to do. Work always consumes me, and when I'm not working, Nacio or Kinsley consume the rest of my time.

"So, how far along are you?"

I think for a moment. "I think thirteen, maybe fourteen weeks."

She frowns. "So, not early enough that you know the sex of the baby yet?"

I shake my head. "No. I'm supposed to go in for a eighteen-week ultrasound. They said they might be able to tell then."

She nods. "Well, we can still have fun coming up with baby names."

I smile and try to think of names. "How about Mason?"

"Not bad. Lily?"

"That's pretty. Caden?"

She wrinkles her nose, which makes me laugh. "Sophia?"

I shake my head. "Benjamin?"

"Nah. Catherine?"

I laugh. "Based on the names we are throwing out, you think this baby is a girl, and I think it is a boy."

She laughs, too. "I guess so."

I grab her head and pull her toward my lap so that her head is resting on my stomach.

"I can't believe you're pregnant. You're not even showing. You just look like you ate for once. I knew it that day at the Italian restaurant, but you tricked me."

"I know. I'm sorry about that. I just didn't want to cause you pain."

She's silent.

I stroke her hair as she lies on my stomach, and I feel her quickly falling asleep. I lean my head back on the couch and close my eyes. I know I'll be asleep as well soon. We might as well sleep. There is nothing else that we are going to be doing today.

18

BEAST

BORING AFTER BORING day passes until we no longer have to count in days but in weeks. It's been two weeks of living in this nightmare. Two weeks of restless nights, followed by grumpy mornings, where we all just annoy each other until the boredom sets back in.

Despite how big this house is, there isn't much to do here, not when you don't have power or TV or any real sort of entertainment. We have a chessboard and a pool table, but after a few rounds of each, those both become boring. We all smell, as we shower only every few days.

I bought battery operated security cameras to monitor the property twenty-four/seven. That's where I spend most of my day, monitoring the cameras and tweaking where they point, even though all I ever see on them is the occasional bunny or squirrel.

I also make excuses to go into town to pick up supplies and check messages on my phone. Each time I do, I hope that Reina has called and is ready to put an end to this. Instead, the messages are always from them. They think they can solve this, but they can't.

After the first day, I brought Scarlett and Kinsley into town, so they could call Killian and Preston and let them know that they are safe but not coming home for a while. Now, they want to go into town with me every chance they get. I do the best to keep them at home where it is safer. They don't realize that what I'm really hoping is that Reina will show herself to me here, and then I can put a stop to this. That never happens though.

Instead of coming with me, Scarlett and Kinsley spend most of their days talking with each other about the baby. Baby clothes, baby cribs, baby things that I didn't even know existed.

I've barely even spent time with Scarlett these past two weeks. And, with each day that passes, I feel Scarlett slipping further and further away.

Scarlett wants Kinsley in her life, not me. Kinsley would be better with the baby than me. And Scarlett knows that we both can't be in her life. Despite being cordial to each other, Kinsley and I haven't exactly grown closer.

That's partially why I'm so annoyed that I haven't figured out a plan to stop Reina. To put an end to this, so we can figure out what our lives are going to be like after this.

"She's slipping away, you know," Santino says from behind me.

I pull the staple remover from my bag. I should have removed the staples a few days ago, but it didn't even cross my mind. My arm has healed as good as can be expected, and now that the pain is gone, I barely think about it anymore.

"Is that meant to be a motivational speech or something?" I begin pulling the staples out of my arm. It burns a little as I rip out a few arm hairs and skin that has begun to grow over the staples since I left them in for too long.

Santino chuckles. "I can see why Scarlett likes you, you being so pleasant and all."

I pull out a staple and toss it on the table, ignoring him.

"We can't keep doing this forever, you know. At some point, we are going to have to go on the offensive or at least talk to Reina. We can't keep hiding forever."

I nod. I agree with him. I'm just trying to come up with a plan that doesn't involve me having to put a bullet between Reina's eyes.

"I know," Santino says even though I didn't say anything. He knows what I was going to say. He feels the same way. "I'm going to go pester Kinsley. She's always fun to annoy."

"We are supposed to be trying to get Kinsley to like us."

Santino laughs. "No. You are supposed to be trying to get Kinsley to like you. I'm not the one trying to fuck her best friend."

"Fucking," I correct him.

He stops at the door to the patio. "Uh-huh. I haven't noticed any of that going on since we got here."

"It's not exactly what's on my mind when I'm trying to protect us all."

"Sure, whatever you say, Nacio. Just know that I meant what I said. We can't keep doing this forever. Our time here is coming to an end, and you need to remind Scarlett why she fell for you in the first place."

"Which is?"

He laughs. "I assume the fucking." He opens the door and then shouts, "I think Nacio needs help with his staples, Beauty!"

I glare at him when he calls her Beauty for the millionth time even though I've asked him to stop the same number of times. He enjoys getting to me, which I allow him to do every time he uses my name for her.

Scarlett walks into the kitchen, and when she sees all the staples are out, she glances down at my arm in confusion. "Santino said you needed help with the staples?"

"Santino thought wrong."

"Oh, okay." Scarlett bites her lip. She glances back at Kinsley and Santino out on the deck and then turns back to me as a slow smile curls up. "Fuck me," she says.

I raise an eyebrow at her, not sure I heard her right.

She laughs at my expression. "Fuck me."

She walks toward me, and my eyes grow heavy, needing to see her naked body that can no longer hide the baby in her stomach. Her breasts have swelled, and she's never looked more beautiful. Despite the sweatpants and tank top that she is wearing, she's beautiful.

I swallow the thought down though. I let her suck me off in this house before, but now, all I can think about is keeping her safe and trying to keep the memories of this house that haunt me at bay. I'm too afraid to fuck her for real in this house.

"I need to check a camera out front again. I think a cord came loose." I get up and begin walking toward the door.

Scarlett grabs my arm, and I stop and look at her, my eyes showing the demons that haunt me. I show her that we can't do this. I can't do this.

She doesn't take no for an answer though. She kisses me. But I can't even focus on the kiss. Instead, I grab her wrists and slowly push her away from me.

"I can't."

Scarlett narrows her eyes as her hand touches my face.

I glance away, but every time I do, another memory haunts me—Reina's screams, my father's voice. I can't let my mind go any darker. If I do, I'll never recover.

She sees it all though. "Fuck me."

I don't answer her. She already knows that I can't. I can't fuck her. I'm too afraid that the past memories in this house would mix with current memories and ruin any chance of us staying together.

She takes my hand. "Fine, let's just eat then."

I let her guide me back to the kitchen even though I don't understand why she's okay with going from wanting to fuck to wanting to eat, but she's pregnant, so I'm not going to question her.

"What do you want to eat?" I ask.

"I want to eat some of the cake Santino bought to satisfy my sweet-tooth cravings."

I nod and get the cake out of the pantry. I search for a knife to cut the cake, but Scarlett doesn't bother with a knife. Instead, she sticks her finger into the icing and then slowly brings it to her lips, slowly sucking on it.

I freeze, watching her tongue lick her bottom lip that is still covered in icing. She repeats the motion of licking her finger clean of the frosting, but this time, she lets out the softest moan possible. I'm not even sure I heard it.

"I know what you are doing," I say.

She cocks her head to the side as she runs her finger across her bottom lip. "I'm not doing anything, just eating." She sticks her finger back in the frosting and then holds it up to my lips. "Want some?"

I suck in a breath.

But then she doesn't give me a choice as her finger moves to my lips. I take her finger into my mouth, sucking gently until all the frosting is gone. She closes her eyes and moans.

When I release her finger, she scoops up more frosting,

and I watch as some of it falls from her hand to the peak of her breast.

I lose it.

My lips suck the frosting from her breast as I push her backward, needing our bodies pressed together. I keep pushing backward until one of the windows behind her stops us.

I suck on her breast long after the frosting is gone.

"Fuck me," she whispers in my ear. "Fuck me here, against the drapes on this window."

God, I love my dirty girl. The white drapes are thin, basically see-through, and Santino and Kinsley are sitting out on the deck where they could glance over at this window at any second. That's what she wants though. She seeks the danger, just like I do.

"My pleasure, Beauty."

I lift her hands high above her head, holding them in one hand. My other hand reaches under her tank and moves it higher until it covers her eyes. I watch her mouth part and pant. She needs me as desperately as I need her.

I rip the shirt off her body and toss it on the floor. I unhook her bra and toss it next. Still holding her hands above her head, I have to take a step back to get a good look at her body.

"You're beautiful, Beauty."

She drinks in my words, and for a second, our eyes connect like we haven't done in days.

I hear furniture being scooted on the patio outside, and it reminds me that there is a time limit. We can't take our time if we don't want Santino or Kinsley to catch us. Not that I'd give a fuck if they did. I want them to catch us. I want them to see how I love this woman. Maybe then

Kinsley would realize that I would do anything to protect Scarlett.

I spin her around, pressing her against the thin veil of fabric and glass that is doing nothing to hide her naked breasts from Santino's or Kinsley's sight.

My hand tangles in her hair as I press myself against her body, and my lips kiss her ear. "They could see you." I grab ahold of one of her swollen breasts. "They could see your perfect breasts." I rub her nipple between my fingers and am rewarded with a gasp. "Or your face when you come."

"I don't care. I need you to fuck me."

That's all I need to hear.

I pull my cock out as fast as I can while I kiss her neck and rub her breast. Thank God I don't need to wear a condom anymore because I don't think I'd have time to stop and put one on. She has me so wound up that I can't wait another second to have her and remind her that she's still mine.

Mine to protect, to love.

I slip her pants down, revealing her perfect ass, as I push my cock against it.

I feel her melt a little against my touch, begging me to get inside her.

"I will, Beauty. Patience."

She growls. "I need you now, Beast."

My cock pushes at her entrance, and I feel her wetness covering me, showing me how ready she is.

I glance up and see that Santino and Kinsley aren't paying us any attention. Scarlett turns her head and I kiss her again to show her that I'm still here with her instead of lost in my haunted memories. All I see and feel is her.

I quickly push inside her without warning and listen to her gasp.

I continue to fuck her against the drapes and glass.

It's a feeling I will never get enough of. I will never get enough of her, and guessing from the sounds leaving her mouth and throat, she can't get enough of me either.

Scarlett screams louder than she should, and I place my hand over her mouth to quiet her. I watch as Kinsley turns her head a little toward us.

"Don't move, Beauty. Don't make a sound. She'll see you if you do." While telling her that she has to be silent so that Kinsley doesn't see us, I reach down between her legs, rubbing her clit hard and fast, torturing her by bringing her so close to coming.

I feel her about to come, so I meet her there until we are both silently coming as our mouths connect to keep us both silent. Her eyes are closed, but my eyes are open, watching her. Then, I glance past her. Kinsley peeks over at us for just a second, and I see the flush of pink on her cheeks.

Good, maybe now she'll realize that I love Scarlett.

I frown. *Or she'll think I'm just using her friend for sex.*

Scarlett collapses in my arms, clearly exhausted. I scoop her up along with her clothes and carry her to the couch. I dress her as she smiles at me.

"Did I get rid of your demons?" she asks.

I nod. "When I'm with you, I can't think of anything else but you."

"Good."

She holds out her arms, and I pull her tank top down over her body before grabbing a throw blanket and covering her.

"Stay," she says when I stand back up.

I grin. "One second."

I walk back to the dining room to put the cake away, but I stop in my tracks when I see a man standing in the hallway. I immediately reach for my gun because I'm sure he's here to kill me. There is no other reason he would be here but to get his wife back and he'll kill me to do that. But I'm not going to be the one who fires the first shot. I'm not going to kill Killian if I don't have to.

19

SCARLETT

"Where's my wife?" I hear a man say from the hallway.

I quickly get up off the couch because I know that voice.

But I still can't believe it when I make it to the hallway and see Killian standing there.

"What are you doing here?" I ask even though I know it's a stupid question.

The more important question is, *How did he find us?*

Because, if he could find us, that means that Reina can, too.

He doesn't answer my first question, and I don't get to ask my second. Instead, I hear the can't-believe-it scream from Kinsley behind me before she rushes into Killian's arms.

I glance over at Nacio, who has his hand on his gun in the back of his pants. I'm surprised he doesn't have it out.

If I thought the display that Nacio and I just did against the window was embarrassing, Kinsley and Killian's display of affection is almost just as bad. They kiss as their hands go all over each other's bodies. Grabbing things that I don't

149

want to see grabbed. Making sounds that I don't want to hear coming from my best friend and her husband.

I clear my throat, trying to remind them that we are all still standing here, but they don't acknowledge that they heard me at all. They just keep kissing and feeling each other up.

Santino laughs from behind me. "You don't have much room to talk. Don't think we didn't see you two going at it against the window."

My hand goes up to cover my gaping mouth. "You saw what?"

This just makes Santino laugh harder.

I turn my shocked expression to Nacio, who is just shaking his head like it doesn't matter. He knew. He knew that they could see us, and he didn't stop. He didn't pull me away from the window. He just let them watch. They probably heard my screams, too.

I cross my arms over my chest, annoyed with Nacio and Santino for embarrassing me. Not that I'm that embarrassed, but it's still not something I wanted them to see. I just liked the idea of possibly getting caught.

Kinsley and Killian finally stop kissing and turn to look at us. Nacio slowly lets go of his gun when he sees that Killian is holding on to Kinsley with a smile on his face.

"You might not want to let go of your gun. If I can find you, then Reina can, too. What sort of protection do you have set up here?" Killian says to Nacio.

Nacio looks to Killian in surprise. "I have security cameras set up on every inch to warn us if Reina sends any more men after us along with plenty of weapons to protect us."

Killian nods and smiles. "Good."

Kinsley looks up at her husband in confusion, just like

I'm looking at them. "Why aren't you trying to rip Nacio's head off right now?"

Killian quickly kisses his wife on the lips. "Because he's one of the good guys."

Kinsley's mouth drops as she looks from her husband to Nacio to me. I shake my head. I have no idea what he is talking about.

I look at Nacio, who is frozen, not letting on about anything either.

"What do you mean, he's one of the good guys?" I ask Killian because I don't trust Nacio to give me a straight answer.

Killian cocks his head to the side, like he can't believe that Nacio hasn't shared the one good thing about himself with me. "He works for the FBI."

Kinsley looks at Nacio. "How is that possible?"

Nacio just stares at her but doesn't answer, so she turns back to her husband.

"He was given an opportunity to work for the FBI in exchange for his freedom from prison. In fact, since he's gotten out, he's had a hand in helping the FBI take down several career criminals."

I turn to look at Nacio. I'm trying to understand how he works for the FBI, knowing the things he's done.

Out of the corner of my eye, I see Santino, and he looks just as shocked as the rest of us.

"So, you've turned to the good side." Kinsley glances at me then back to Nacio. "Maybe I can accept your relationship with my friend after all."

Nacio still hasn't said anything, not one word since Killian began speaking. I try to read Nacio's face, but I can't. I try to understand why he hasn't spoken, but I can't.

The first movement Nacio finally makes is to shake his

head, and then he screams in terror as he reaches back to pull his gun.

A loud popping sound rings out. A sound that I have learned to associate with gunfire.

I hear screaming, but I can't make out what anyone is saying. I crouch down, protecting my head, as bullets fly overhead.

Killian might not have meant to, but he brought Reina's men with him. He showed her our location, and now, the house is under attack by who knows how many people.

I search the room, trying to decide on what to do or where to go. But all I see is chaos.

Hands wrap around me, and I jump and let out a scream until I realize it's Nacio.

"We have to go," he says, pushing me forward, as he fires a shot over my head.

I scream again. I can't help it.

"Now, Scarlett." He pushes me forward, and then we are running, but I have no idea where.

He pushes me toward what I think is the garage, and I scream as I see a gun is pointed at us from around the corner. Nacio pushes me behind him as he fires his gun. I watch every bullet that flies by our heads, afraid that any single one could end either of our lives.

The gunshots don't stop, so I pull Nacio back, trying to get him to retreat away from the gun in front of us, hoping that if we move away we will be safe. He holds me firmly while firing another shot that ends the gunshots raining down on us.

He grabs my arm and then marches us forward with his gun in his hand. This time, instead of running, we walk slowly and carefully, assuming someone else is going to run out and attack. I don't know whether to keep my eyes on Nacio or on what's ahead of us. But, if I'm going to die by a bullet, I would rather keep my eyes on Nacio. I do but realize that keeping my eyes on him doesn't ensure his protection. I must do something to help protect him, and watching him is doing nothing.

"I need a gun," I say.

He glances at me like I'm crazy but then realizes that giving me a gun is the only thing he can do. While we've been here, he should have spent time teaching me how to shoot. Instead, he hoped that he would be able to fight them off without me.

He reaches down by his ankle and produces another gun that he hands to me. I take the gun. It feels strange in my hand. It's the first time I've ever held a gun.

Nacio places his hands over mine, quickly showing me how to hold the gun. "Just keep your eyes open and only shoot if you have to."

I nod.

We keep moving forward, passing the body of the man who was firing at us. I don't look down as we step over him. I don't want to give this man the satisfaction of haunting my dreams.

We make our way to the garage. Nacio opens the door and then quickly looks around, holding out his gun, before he allows me to enter. We move quickly to the car as Nacio digs out a key and presses a button that turns on the remote start.

But the car doesn't start.

"Damn it!" Nacio runs to the hood of the car and pops it open. "They've taken the battery."

He grabs me and pulls me back toward the door that leads back into the house.

"Stay close behind me. I'm going to get you out of here safely."

"What about everyone else?"

"Killian is more than capable of watching out for Kinsley, and Santino will do fine by himself. They might have already put an end to this by the time we make our way back into the house."

I take a deep breath, hoping his words are true.

But in case they aren't...

I kiss him without thinking. He kisses me back, letting the kiss go on for far too long. Neither of us cares though. This could be our last kiss, and we are going to make it memorable if it is.

Nacio finally forces our lips apart and tightly grabs my hand before he quietly leads me back into the house. We slink silently down the halls, but as we grow closer to the main living area, we can hear it. Gunshots are ringing in every direction.

Nacio looks into my eyes, and I can see the indecisiveness there. He's trying to decide if I would be safer with him or staying out of the line of fire.

"I'm coming with you."

He doesn't agree or disagree. He just moves again, and I follow. I firmly hold my gun, despite my shaking hands. And I keep my eyes glued on what is in front of us, knowing that I can no longer think about Nacio. I have to focus on keeping us both alive.

I move with Nacio as he stealthily makes his way, following the shadows, without being seen. He sees a man around the corner and fires multiple shots at him. I didn't see him until it was already too late. The man falls to the ground before he even gets a shot off.

We creep forward to the edge of the hallway.

"Stay here," he whispers without looking at me.

He takes a step out into the line of fire and begins quickly shooting in multiple directions while I cower against the wall, petrified. I think I see Kinsley and Killian taking cover behind some cabinets in the kitchen. Otherwise, all I see is Nacio and bullets flying.

I hold my gun up, prepared to shoot, but I have no idea what I'm doing. I can't see anyone but Nacio. So, I just stay frozen where I am with my eyes locked on his body.

I see it happen. I see him get hit in maybe his chest or his stomach. I can't tell from where I am, but wherever he was hit, it's not good.

I don't think. I just react.

I run forward, needing to make sure that he is okay. I keep my gun up, trying my best to scan from side to side to keep myself out of danger, while all I'm thinking about is how he can't die.

I reach him, wrapping my arms around him, trying to protect him from any more harm, while searching for where he was hit. I can't find it though, and he is trying to drag me away to somewhere he can keep me safe.

I won't let him go though because I can tell in the way that he is moving me that he isn't safe. He's hurting worse than when the shot hit him in the arm. And I will not leave him alone to suffer in pain and likely die.

I glance up behind him, and I see a man. His gun is aimed at Nacio's head. He'll never turn around in time. He'll never move in time to get out of the way of the bullet.

I squeeze the trigger of my gun that is already aimed in his direction. I fire over and over again as I scream, begging the world to not let him die.

The man drops in a similar fashion to the one Nacio shot. And then the room is silent.

Nacio gently pulls me away from his body so that he can look at me, making sure I'm not hurt. He then quickly glances around the room and makes a motion to Santino, who nods in agreement.

We are safe—at least at the moment.

I touch Nacio's chest and find the wound. I exhale all my air when I realize that the wound is superficial, even less so than the one on his arm. It must have just knocked the wind out of him.

"Damn it, Scarlett. I should punish you for being so stupid. You could have died."

"You could have, too."

He kisses me again, sucking all the air from my lungs, making me dizzy with each kiss but not caring in the slightest.

We are all alive.

Even though this will not be the last battle we have to fight, it is the last battle for the moment.

Pain shoots through my head. The room spins so much that I can't even see Nacio standing right in front of me. I don't even know if I'm in his arms anymore.

I hear him and others shouting my name.

I hear, "Scarlett," and, "Scar," and, "Beauty," all ringing in the air.

But I can't answer any of them.

20

BEAST

I LET Scarlett go for just one second. Just one fucking second.

And, because I let her go, she's gone.

She fell to the floor before I could grab her. The memory will haunt me forever and be far worse than the demons of my past. Everything moved in slow motion when she fell, but even still, I couldn't do anything to stop her from falling. I couldn't save her.

"Beauty!" I scream. I drop to my knees to protect her from whoever is shooting, but I don't hear the sound of a gun firing, and I didn't before.

I hear Kinsley scream as she runs over along with Killian and Santino. We all surround Scarlett, searching for the wound that caused her to fall. But I can't find it.

"Scarlett! Beauty! Wake up!"

She doesn't move.

I place my head on her chest and find her breathing. She's alive.

"I don't know what's wrong with her!" I shout to the others.

Kinsley is already kneeling next to me and is searching Scarlett's body. She looks at me, and she doesn't know what's wrong either. "We need to get her to a hospital."

I nod even though I hate hospitals. There are too many questions in hospitals. People in hospitals just get sicker; they don't get better. But I don't know how to make Scarlett better. I don't know what's wrong.

I scoop her up, and Kinsley screams as she grabs at Scarlett's head. I see the blood on Kinsley's hands from the wound on Scarlett's head, and then I'm afraid.

"Santino, get the gauze!" I shout.

He does and quickly comes back. Kinsley grabs it and applies it to Scarlett's head.

Then, we both run toward the front door without saying a word to each other. We don't argue or fight. We just help save a woman we both love.

We run through the door with me holding Scarlett's body and Kinsley applying pressure to her head. I spot what I hope is Killian's black SUV. We get to the doors that are unlocked and climb in the backseat.

"Go!" Kinsley and I both shout to Killian at the same time as he jumps in the driver's seat.

Santino gets in on the passenger side.

Killian steps on it and quickly makes his way down the drive. Santino already has the address of the nearest hospital pulled up on his phone.

I squeeze Scarlett's hand. "Just hold on, Beauty. We are going to get you some help. Just stay alive, like you promised. You and your baby both, please just stay alive."

Kinsley looks at me with tears in her eyes and then back to Scarlett's head. I can see the blood soaking through the gauze.

"Head wounds always look like there is more blood than there actually is."

Kinsley nods.

"Keep applying pressure."

I glance up to Santino. "Did you bring more gauze?"

"Sorry, that's all we had."

I pull my shirt off and hand it to Kinsley. "Put the shirt on top of the gauze to soak up the remaining blood. Don't remove the gauze. Just apply the shirt on top of it."

She does, and I keep looking until I'm satisfied that she is applying enough pressure. I realize that she is looking at me, staring at my body, and then she glances up to meet Killian's eyes in the rearview mirror. I watch the exchange in confusion.

"I can see why Scarlett likes you," Kinsley says.

I cock my head to look at her. "Why?"

"For one, you are far more loving and caring than I thought possible."

I nod, squeezing Scarlett's hand harder, willing her to wake up.

"And, two, you are one sexy beast."

I can't help but smile at her words. I don't know if Scarlett has told Kinsley her nickname for me or what, but I finally feel like I have her approval to date her best friend. I just hope it's not too late.

I know Killian is driving as fast as he can, but I just need him to drive faster. Every second that goes by is another second that I risk losing her.

I finally see a hospital coming into view.

"Just hold on, Beauty. We are almost there. Just a couple of more minutes."

Killian pulls over to the emergency side of the hospital, and Santino pops out before we have even stopped. He opens my door, and I begin to slide out with Scarlett still in my lap. Kinsley slides with me, still applying pressure to her head.

I'm finally out of the car with Scarlett in my hands, and I wait just a second for Kinsley to get out while holding her head. Then, we both race inside to the counter of the emergency room.

The nurse behind the desk doesn't ask us any silly insurance questions. She just presses a button on her pager and calls for a doctor immediately. "What happened?"

"I don't know. She just collapsed, and I think she hit her head," I say.

Doctors and nurses rush in with a gurney that they instruct me to put her on. I do, and Kinsley reluctantly lets go of her head as a nurse takes over.

"She's pregnant!" I shout over the noise.

"How far along?"

"I don't fucking know."

"I think sixteen, maybe seventeen weeks," Kinsley says.

The nurse nods.

And then I see them start to take Scarlett back into the ER, away from me. When I brought her here, I knew that was what would happen, that they wouldn't let me back to be by her side. Still, it kills me to see her leave. I walk behind her as they push her back behind the doors until one of them puts a hand up to stop me, and I stop.

"I love you. You're going to be okay!" I shout as the door shuts in my face.

I turn to see Kinsley standing right next to me, doing the same thing. She's just as helpless as I am. Neither of us has any idea of what could be wrong with Scarlett. Neither of us knows if she is going to live or die. Neither of us has any control over what is going to happen to her next, despite that we'd both be willing to give our own lives to protect hers and her baby's.

Instead, all we have left of her in the moment is each other. To my surprise, Kinsley steps toward me, and I'm afraid she's going to lecture me, tell me that this is exactly why I can't date Scarlett. That I'm putting her life in danger every day that I'm with her.

Instead, Kinsley wraps her arms around me. I gently lower my arms and wrap them around her. I can feel her tears on my bare chest.

"Thank you," she says when she pulls away.

"You don't have anything to thank me for."

She smiles. "You saved her life."

I shake my head but don't argue with her. Now is not the time.

She studies my chest where a bullet scratched the surface of my skin causing a small wound. "You should have them look at that."

"No, I'm fine. I need to be here when there is news about her, and I don't want anyone to know that we were being shot at."

I see Santino and Killian walk over. Santino tosses me a clean shirt that he must have just bought in the gift shop. I put it on, and then we each take a seat in the waiting room and wait.

21

SCARLETT

I WAKE up to a pounding headache and four sets of eyes staring at me. I try to sit up, but Nacio and Kinsley both stop me on each side of my bed.

"What happened?" I ask, holding my pounding forehead.

"You passed out, Scar. Just a drop in blood pressure. You're going to be perfectly fine," Kinsley says.

I hate to even ask her, but I have to know. "And the baby?"

She smiles through her tears. "She is perfectly fine."

"It's a she?"

She nods and squeezes me tightly. Nacio hugs me as well, and then Killian and Santino join in on the fun. I don't know what happened while I was asleep, but somehow, everyone came together, much closer together than I ever thought possible.

Is there hope that our two worlds could survive together?

I wince a little when someone's arm accidentally collides with my head, and everyone moves off of me.

"Why does my head hurt so much?"

"When you passed out, you hit your head," Nacio says.

I can see the pain in his eyes. He thinks this is his fault. Although, if all I have is a cut on my head, I think I will be fine. He did what he could to save me.

A woman that I assume is a doctor comes in. "You're awake. How are you feeling?"

"Tired, and my head hurts."

"That's to be expected. Do you all mind giving me and Scarlett a few minutes alone, so I can do an exam?"

Killian and Santino immediately leave, giving me tight smiles before exiting my hospital room. But Nacio and Kinsley both stand firm on either side of my bed.

The doctor smiles. "I promise, I will let you both back in as soon as the exam is done. I just want to check her over again and give her an update on her condition."

"We aren't leaving," Nacio says.

The doctor looks to me.

"I'm really okay with them both staying."

The doctor frowns. "Fine."

She begins talking about my condition. It was just a drop in my blood pressure, and I should be fine going forward.

"You were probably just dehydrated," she says.

I nod, not letting on that stress probably caused the dizziness. She talks more, and I hear something about needing to stay overnight for observation.

"Scarlett? Scarlett, did you hear me?" the doctor asks.

"Yes. Sorry, what did you say?"

The doctor begins flashing a light in my eyes, and then after a moment, she seems satisfied that there is nothing wrong. I just wasn't listening very well. Instead, I was thinking about what a future would be like with all of us.

The doctor interrupts those thoughts again, "Would you like to see your baby?"

I smile. "Yes."

She brings in the ultrasound tech, and she begins setting everything up. She rubs cold gel on my swollen stomach, and before I realize it, a picture of my baby girl is on the screen. Nacio and Kinsley each squeeze my hand.

"She's beautiful," Kinsley says, sighing.

"Just like her mother," Nacio says.

I study the beautiful picture of the baby that is still thriving in my stomach, despite everything I have put her through.

"It's a girl? That's what I was told," I ask the technician.

"Yep. It's definitely a girl."

I smile. *A girl.*

The technician prints off some pictures and hands one to me and one to Nacio. "You two are going to make great parents. I can always tell the ones who are prepared from the ones who don't have their stuff together. You two are going to do great. You even have the support of great friends. I'll leave you alone now." The technician wipes the gel off my stomach before she walks out.

I frown because the technician has it all wrong. We aren't going to make great parents.

"Kinsley, do you mind giving Nacio and me some time alone? Just for a few minutes. You can go show the pictures to the guys."

She nods. "Of course." She leans down and kisses my cheek. "I'm so happy you are both okay."

And then she leaves me and Nacio alone in my hospital room. I wipe the remnants of gel off my stomach, that the tech missed, with a towel and then pull my hospital gown back down, so I don't feel so exposed.

Nacio gently strokes my hair as he sits next to me. "When you collapsed...I've never felt so afraid in my life. I'm so sorry. I should have caught you. I shouldn't have put you under that much risk. I should have protected you better than I did. I failed you."

"Shh...no, you didn't. You saved me, protected me. I'm fine, and the baby is fine. There is nothing more you could have done."

"I could have caught you."

I shake my head. "It doesn't matter. We are both here. We are all alive. That's all that matters."

He smiles and touches my stomach. "That was amazing."

"What was?"

"Seeing your baby on the screen. It was incredible."

"It was, wasn't it?"

He nervously looks down at his hand on my stomach. "I know we haven't talked much about what our future looks like or if a future together is even possible."

I nod. "I know there are so many things to figure out. One thing that seems to have straightened itself out is you and Kinsley."

"Yeah, I think she's finally come around to the idea of us."

"Good. I'm glad."

"I know we have a lot to figure out. Our lifestyles. Our jobs. I have a lot of explaining to do about my involvement with the FBI."

I nod.

"But, after seeing that picture of your baby, I don't think I could ever *not* be in your baby's life again. I know I'm not the actual father, but I can't imagine not being a father to your baby."

I frown. "Nacio...we need to talk about the baby. There are some things you need to know."

"All I need to know is that I love you and this baby"—he rubs his hand across my stomach again—"more than anything else."

"I know. But I need to tell you—"

He shuts me up with a tender kiss, making my words disappear just as easily as they came. I don't have thoughts until he pulls away and says, "I'm going to put a stop to this. I'm going to keep you safe. I'm not going to let anything happen to you or your baby."

"What do you mean?"

"I'm going to go talk with Reina. I'm going to end this."

I grab his arm. "No, just wait until I can leave the hospital, and we will go together."

"No, this is my battle. You need to stay here and protect our baby."

I love the sound when he says *our* baby.

"Stay here. You can turn her into the FBI. They can arrest her and put a stop to this."

He freezes, not ready to have this conversation with me, but he has to. "I'm not really a good guy, Beauty. You had me pegged the second you called me Beast."

"I know," is all I say because I know he doesn't have loyalties to the FBI.

The FBI might think he works for them, is loyal to them, but he's not. The FBI would never have been okay with him killing everyone he's killed.

"And, as much as I want to be a good husband, a good father, I'm none of those things. Not until I protect my family and set things right. Not until I become the good guy that the FBI, Killian, and Kinsley think I am."

"Nacio."

But he's already pulling away. He's already made up his mind. He's leaving me, and there is nothing I can do to stop him.

I grab his neck and pull him to me to kiss him, hoping that I can get him to stop thinking about risking his life to try to save mine. Instead, I want him to do whatever it takes to stay here with me.

He kisses me. And I think for a moment that there is no way he will be able to leave me after this kiss.

His lips move off of mine, and then he turns around so that he can't see me.

"Nacio! Wait."

He doesn't wait. He walks out the door, leaving me all alone.

I look around the room for my cell phone, but I don't see it anywhere. I find the Call button to call my nurse or doctor and press it over and over.

I consider getting out of bed and going after him, but I still have an IV in my arm. And wires are hooked up to my chest, monitoring my vitals. As much as I love Nacio, I can't risk the baby's health just to try to stop him. I doubt I would be able to stop him anyway.

A nurse rushes in. "Are you okay? Can I get you anything?"

"Sorry, I just need my friend Kinsley to come in. I'm sorry. I don't know where my phone is or any other way to get ahold of her."

She frowns. "I'll see if I can find her for you."

She leaves, and then I'm all alone.

If he thinks that leaving me here while he's putting himself at risk is helping to protect me, he's wrong. Because I'm sure my blood pressure has risen higher than what is safe. He's putting me in just as much risk while I wait here for him to come back.

Kinsley walks in the door. "Are you okay?"

"No."

"I'll grab a doctor. Hold on."

"No, wait. I'm physically fine. Nacio left. He's going to go see his sister to try to put a stop to this."

She nods. "I know. He told me before he left."

"And you let him go?"

"Yes, he needs to put a stop to this, Scarlett."

I sigh. "He doesn't know the full truth about the baby."

Thank God there is a chair behind her because she doesn't even look when she sits down. "He doesn't know?"

"No."

"So, he thinks..."

"Yep."

"He thinks he's protecting his future child by doing this, doesn't he?"

I nod. "That's why I can't let him do this. As much as he wants this child to be his and as much as I know he would make a great father and take care of it like it were his own, you know that this baby can never be his. He doesn't deserve to die for a child that can never be his."

"He's not going to die."

I take a deep breath. "He doesn't deserve to risk his life either."

Kinsley nods. "I'm sorry."

"It's not your fault. Just help me get out of here, so I can stop him. I love him, Kinsley. He can't die."

She nods again. "I'll help you."

22

BEAST

I OPEN the door to Reina's house in Chicago. I know she's here. I tracked her cell.

The whole way here, I should have been thinking of ways to convince Reina to stop this. Instead, all I could think about was Scarlett. How I want a normal, boring life with her where we can raise her baby together and not have to worry about who is coming after us to kill us. That's all I want.

But I'm not sure if, even after I convince Reina to stop trying to kill Scarlett and Kinsley, that is going to happen.

Scarlett wanted to tell me something about the baby. Most likely, the baby girl's father. I didn't want to hear it though. Not when I knew I needed to come here and protect her and her baby. I didn't want to hear that she'd decided to be with her baby's father.

Since I've spent time worrying about a future that I will likely never have, I have zero ideas on how to convince Reina to change her mind.

I walk in with my gun raised, prepared to shoot anyone

who fucking works for Reina. I walk through the house and straight to Reina's office.

"Done killing my best men?" Reina says, not even bothering to look up from her computer screen.

I walk into her office with my gun still drawn. "I'm not done until your men are done coming after Scarlett and Kinsley."

"Why? Because you've gone soft on me and don't want to kill innocent women anymore? Please."

"No, because I love her."

She laughs. "She doesn't love you back. She got knocked up by some other guy."

"That was when she thought I was a monster. I'm not a monster anymore, Reina. I want to do better."

"You will never be anything else. You're holding a fucking gun in my face. I'm your sister. How does that not make you a monster?"

I don't lower my gun. I don't let her get to me.

"Reina, this has to stop. Just let it go, and move on. I love Scarlett. That's all you need to know to stop the hit you put out on her and Kinsley."

She cocks her head. "Nothing is going to stop the hit on Kinsley. She has to die. Showing that we don't take kindly to traitors is the only way anyone will respect my company and not walk all over us. And Scarlett doesn't love you back. Just let me kill her and put you out of your misery."

"Stop it," I say, walking toward her. "I don't care if Scarlett loves me back or not. I love her, so that's enough for you to put a stop to the hit."

"No. I love you, Nacio. I care about you. And I'm not going to let a bitch like her destroy your life. Just let me do my job."

I grab one of the chairs in her office and throw it hard

against the wall. "You're not listening to me, Reina. I'm not asking you. I'm telling you what to do. I'm the one with the gun. I can kill you right here and take over the company if I wanted to."

She laughs. "You wouldn't kill me. I'm your sister. You've spent your entire life protecting me after you fucked up when we were kids."

I frown. "You're right. I did protect you. I've always protected you, and I'm sick of it. You don't get to keep hanging that over my head anymore. Not after you told me the truth."

"You don't know how to stop protecting me, Nacio. It's the only good part of you."

"Maybe I just want to protect someone who deserves it for a change."

She nods slowly. "Maybe, or maybe it's because you don't have the balls to just kill her like she deserves for getting knocked up by another man, especially this man in particular."

"Enough, Reina." I tighten my grip on the gun as I point it at her.

She smiles. "Just trying to help my brother out since she obviously hasn't told you who the father is yet."

I freeze. I don't want to know how she knows, and I don't want to hear it.

"Killian's the father, Nacio. She let that bastard fuck her and knock her up." She studies her nails. "I guess since he couldn't knock up his wife, he felt the need to spread his sperm around with any woman who would fuck him."

"You're lying."

She smiles as she looks back up at me. "Am I? Hmm...I guess you'll never know because that tramp will never tell you the truth."

"I should kill you," I say.

"You won't though. You should kill Scarlett and Kinsley. They are the ones who have betrayed you, not me."

"You don't get it, do you, Reina? I own you. I've been working with the FBI, but I've been doing it to protect you. I've turned in your enemies instead of you to the FBI. I've steered them away from you anytime they caught your scent and picked up your trail. I made sure you stayed alive. If you betray me, that's over. I'll turn you over to them...if I don't kill you."

She shakes her head as her phone buzzes in her pocket. She pulls it out and looks at the screen and then back to me. "That might be true, but in order to make threats like that, you have to have all the cards."

Reina glances past me, and my heart stops as I turn to look behind me. One of Reina's men has his arm around Scarlett's neck, his other hand pointing a gun against her temple.

Fuck.

I can't keep my eyes off of Scarlett as he drags her into the room.

I'm sorry, she mouths to me.

I don't mouth or say anything back because I don't know how to get out of this situation. I could save myself and get out of here, but I don't know how to save her. Not without killing Reina.

But I already know Reina's play. She'll force me to put down my gun in order to save Scarlett, and then she will shoot us both. Reina doesn't give a fuck about me any more than she does Scarlett. And, if I'm no longer of value to her, if I'm no longer willing to kill for her, then I'm just a liability that needs to be taken care of.

But, if all three of us are going to die, I want to at least do one thing first that might bring Scarlett and me a tiny bit of happiness before we die.

I slowly lower my gun as I kneel down. I gently place the gun next to my feet and then slide it toward Reina.

"Smart move, Nacio. I knew you would do the right thing."

"I didn't do that for you, Reina. I did it, so I could do this."

I quickly reach into my pocket and produce the box before Reina's goon thinks I could be pulling out another gun.

I look up at Scarlett with a smile on my face because, if this is the last thing I do, it might be the best way to die.

I open the box, displaying a large engagement ring that I had designed weeks ago. I look up at Scarlett, into her glistening eyes that no longer show fear.

"Scarlett Bell, I'm so sorry.

"I'm sorry that I never found the time to ask you this before.

"I'm sorry that I couldn't find a more romantic time or place to do this.

"I'm sorry that it took me forever to admit my feelings for you. To admit that I had more than lust.

"I'm sorry that I didn't take you on enough dates.

"I'm sorry that I didn't have time to study every look on your face and every curve of your body.

"I'm sorry that I never got to spoil you properly like the woman that you are.

"I'm sorry that I never realized until recently how much I wanted your baby to be our baby. How much I wanted to be a family with just the three of us.

"I'm sorry that it took me too long to tell you that I love you.

"I know we don't have much time left, and I want nothing more than to be able to propose and ask you to marry me. And I'm sorry now that we will never get that chance.

"So, instead of asking you to marry me and then never being able to actually get married, I'm going to ask you a different question instead. I'm going to ask you to forgive me for being the beast that I am and ask you to promise that you will love me every second for as long as we both shall live. I love you, Beauty, and I can't imagine a better way to spend what I have left of my life than by looking at your gorgeous eyes when I die."

A tear rolls gently down her cheek, but I don't think it's an unhappy tear or even a tear out of fear. It's pure happiness.

"I'll love you forever even if forever isn't long enough," she says.

23

SCARLETT

I FUCKED UP. I realize that now in hindsight, but when I came here, I thought I would be able to protect Nacio. I thought I could convince Reina to leave us alone. To let us live.

Instead, I'm going to get us both killed instead of just me.

But it's all worth it. To see Nacio down on one knee, proposing to me, is one of the best moments of my life.

Now, it's going to end. I still have a gun pointed at my head, and Nacio doesn't know it, but Reina has a gun pointed at his head. I just hope that, when they kill us, they do it at the same time because I don't want to spend a second of what's left of my life without Nacio in it.

Nacio is still kneeling on the floor, and as much as I want to keep looking into his eyes for the rest of this short life, I haven't given up yet. I can't, not when I have a baby growing inside me.

I look into Reina's eyes. "I love your brother very much. I would never do anything to hurt him. I just want to protect him, just like you do."

I watch Reina lower her gun, and I see the pain and conflict in her eyes, but most of all, I see the love there.

"If you love your brother, then put a stop to this. End this," I plead.

I see Reina giving in. I see her preparing to put an end to this. And then I see her glance to her phone and lift her gun again to Nacio's head.

I don't know how I find the strength or if I just take the man holding me by surprise, but I break free of his hold in time to grab Nacio and protect him from getting shot.

"Please, don't kill him. Just spare him at least. I can die, knowing that he gets to live."

"If you are so worried about him living, then who the hell is this?" Reina thrusts the phone in our faces, but I don't have a clue who the men on the screen are.

"The FBI. They must have followed me here," Nacio says. "You need to get out of here now."

Reina looks at him, and I can see the tears there. "You would still try to help me, despite the fact that I threatened to kill the woman you are desperately in love with?"

"Yes. That's what you do for the people you love. You protect them, even when they don't deserve it."

Reina lowers her gun. "I'm sorry."

"No time for that. We need to get you out of here. Now," Nacio says.

He grabs Reina's hand and begins pulling her out of the office. The man who was holding on to me before at gunpoint has already left. He most likely ran the second that Nacio mentioned the FBI.

"Stay here," Nacio says. "I'll be right back."

For once, I listen to Nacio. I stay in Reina's office, and Nacio takes Reina somewhere she will hopefully be able to escape the FBI. Even though she might deserve it, I don't want her to end up in jail.

I don't want to think about Reina anymore though. I think Nacio and I are safe now. I think Nacio did enough to convince her that she doesn't need to go after Kinsley and me in order to protect Nacio. I think she knows we are on his side.

I walk over and pick up the box that Nacio left on the floor. He never got a chance to actually put the ring on my finger. It's a beautiful ring with little diamonds surrounding the large center one and continuing around the band. It might even be more beautiful than the ring he got me before.

I take the ring out of the box and study it but don't put it on. I want Nacio to be the first one to put the ring on my finger. I look inside the ring, and that's when I see the inscription, *Mine forever*. I smile. Forever just got a lot longer now.

I hear a noise outside the office, and I know the FBI is here. I look at the ring one more time before I step out of the office and come face-to-face with another gun in my face.

I automatically put my hands up. I'm really tired of my life being threatened every few seconds. "My name is Scarlett Bell. Reina, the woman you came here for, was holding me hostage."

The man slowly lowers his gun as he realizes that I'm telling the truth. "Let me get you out of here then."

He grabs ahold of my arm and begins guiding me out of the house. As we walk, I see more men pouring into the house. I just hope they come up empty.

He leads me next to one of their unmarked SUVs. He opens the door for me, and I climb in. "Wait here."

I nod as he shuts the door, and I keep my eyes glued on the door, waiting for Nacio to come back.

It takes a long time for him to emerge, but when he does, the sight I see is not what I expected. An FBI agent has Nacio in handcuffs, leading him to a different door.

I throw the door open and run to him. "What are you doing?" I shout to the FBI agent. "He's innocent."

The man laughs. "This man is anything but innocent."

"He works for you. He was trying to turn his sister over to you."

He shakes his head again. "This man was trying to deceive the FBI—again."

I stop trying to argue with the man. I walk faster until I can see Nacio's eyes one last time before he is shoved into the back of a car. "Nacio..."

"I'm sorry, Beauty. I'm not a good guy. I'm just a beast that never turns back into a man."

I reach out and kiss his lips, shutting him up. The kiss doesn't last long enough though because one of the other FBI agents pulls me off of him. I watch until he is placed in the back of a car and then driven away.

"What will happen to him?" I ask the FBI agent who pulled me off of him.

"He's going to prison for a long time."

"How long?"

"My best guess is life. That was his original sentence that we commuted if he helped us. Instead, he screwed us and probably killed who knows how many other people while he was out. He was never working for us. So, yeah, I think, even if he gets life, he will be getting off easy."

I freeze as I look down at the ring I'm still holding in my hand. Forever isn't such a long time after all.

24

BEAST

PRISON ISN'T such a horrible place. At least not the physical prison I'm in, where I'll most likely be spending the rest of my life. This time, I don't think I will be able to find a way out. The FBI has no reason to let me back out now that I've ruined their trust.

What's worse is what goes on in my head while I'm locked up here. The pain and suffering that comes with never being able to be around those I love.

But this time around, it won't be as bad. This time, I did everything I wanted to do. I saved everyone who needed saving. I saved Scarlett, Kinsley, Reina, and Scarlett's baby. I saved them all, and in turn, they saved me.

I can't be upset that I still have sins to pay for. I wouldn't change anything about these last few months even if it meant I could still be free. I would have rather spent the time I got with Scarlett then to have never gotten any time with her at all and be free.

For the millionth time in the past two months, I sit down at the table with a pen and paper in my hand. I need to write a note to set Scarlett free. I need to write a note to tell her that she needs to go live her life without me. That she needs to be happy. That I know that the baby is Killian's, and if he makes her happy, then I'm happy for her. That I don't judge her for what she did or for hurting her best friend the way that she did. That I hope they can find a way to be happy.

The only problem is, I haven't been able to write any of those words down. Because, once I do, I'm afraid that it is going to be final. That, by writing her this note, I will be giving up and accepting my fate of living a lonely life here in jail while she lives a life without me.

I just can't. I'm too afraid that, once I do, I'll decide my life isn't worth living. But I could never do that to Scarlett. I could never hurt her like that.

"Marlow, come with me," an officer I don't recognize says to me just as I'm about to force myself to write words down on the paper.

I stand and follow. I've learned not to ask questions in jail and to just do as I'm told.

What surprises me though is when he takes me to a room where my lawyer is seated. I'm not supposed to have another meeting with my lawyer for a few weeks.

I sit down at the table across from him as he smiles at me.

"How are you doing?" my lawyer, Wendell, asks.

"Horrible. I'm in prison, most likely for the rest of my life. Why would you even fucking ask me a question like that?"

"Because today is your lucky day."

I narrow my eyes. "And why is that?"

"Because, today, you are getting out of here."

I suck in a breath, trying to remain calm. I've learned to never trust if I'm getting out or not until I'm actually out.

And I think he must have me mixed up with one of his other clients.

"Your friend Killian talked to the FBI on your behalf and convinced them to give you a break. Convinced them that they couldn't honestly expect you to turn in your sister. Reminded them that you had turned in hundreds of other men in your time with them. And, he said, for that, you deserved for them to honor your deal. Plus, there is no evidence that you did any crimes while you were out. Nacio, you're free."

I shake my head. "That doesn't sound like free. That sounds like they want to continue to use me as their puppet."

Wendell frowns. "Maybe so, but at least you will be able to get out of here and go home every night to the woman you love."

I smile because I don't have the heart to tell him that isn't true. That the woman I love is secretly in love with and fucking another man.

True to his word, Wendell has me out of prison within hours of speaking with me. The FBI reminded me of our deal—that I basically have to work for them, but I will no longer be in prison unless I fuck up again.

I see Scarlett as I walk out of the building. I was expecting her. She's probably here to return the ring I gave her that she accepted under duress.

"Can we talk?" she asks.

I nod and then follow her across the street to a nearby park. She sits down on a bench, so I do the same, sitting next to her. She's wearing a gorgeous white dress. It hugs her now-large belly with her baby that she thinks is a secret but is no longer a secret.

"I wanted to give you this," she says, holding out the ring I gave her.

It's just as I suspected.

I take it. "Thanks." I look down at the ring that she will never wear. "You know, we don't need to do this. I understand. You said yes with a gun pointed to your head. And I didn't even ask you to marry me, not technically. Also, you don't need to tell me about the baby. I already know."

She frowns. "I said yes, and I meant it. I want to marry you, Nacio. I want to spend forever with you. I love you. And how do you know anything about the baby?"

"Reina told me that the baby is Killian's, so I understand if you don't want to be with me. That you would rather be with him. He's been on the straight and narrow for a lot longer than I have."

She slaps me.

I look at her in confusion.

"You think I slept with Killian?"

"You didn't?"

She laughs. "No."

"Then, whose baby is it?"

"It's Killian and Kinsley's baby."

"What? How?"

"I agreed to be their surrogate. After I left, I needed to do something good in the world, and helping them have a baby they so desperately wanted felt like that thing.

"The only thing I wanted was for you to understand that this baby wasn't ours. That you couldn't get attached to it because we wouldn't get to keep it. It's theirs."

I smile. "But we will make an awesome aunt and uncle to this baby." I touch her stomach.

She raises her eyebrows. "We will. Does that mean you aren't rescinding your offer to love me forever?"

"I'm not. Although you were the one who gave me the ring back."

"I just wanted you to be the one to put it on my finger."

I smile and get down on one knee in front of her. "Scarlett, my Beauty, will you marry me? Will you spend forever with me even though forever now could be a long time? Even though we don't know what the future holds?"

"Yes. And we do know what the future holds. It is us spending forever loving each other because, in the end, that's what happens. The Beauty and the Beast live happily ever after."

EPILOGUE

SCARLETT

MY HANDS SHAKE a little as I turn the handle on the door to my office at Beautifully Bell. I've been gone a long time. Too long. I haven't stepped foot in this office for months. Close to a year. I took six months off after I gave birth to Kiera, the beautiful baby girl that has brought so much joy to Kinsley and Killian.

I could have easily come back to work months ago. I should have, but I was scared and selfish. I wanted time to enjoy my niece. I wanted time to spend with Nacio. I wanted time to figure our lives out together. And I wanted time to come to terms with the fact that everyone now knows that I'm with Nacio. A beast. A monster. A killer.

I was scared to come to work in a world where everyone thought of my fiancé as a monster. I'm still scared. But I need to go back to work. I've been gone long enough and it's been torture not working. Well the last couple of months have been torture. I enjoyed the first few months with my niece and Nacio. But that slowly turned to boredom and then torture. I love my work. I love creating clothing and

187

makeup that makes women look and feel beautiful. I love the control. I love pushing myself each day.

I turn the knob and walk into my office. It looks exactly the same but also different at the same time. Nothing has changed, all of my furniture has stayed the exact same, but I've changed. That's the difference.

I walk over to my desk and remove my coat and smile as I notice the small box sitting on my desk. I pick up the note that is attached and open it.

JUST BECAUSE I'M the Beast doesn't mean I'm the strong one. You have more strength than anyone I know. Now go use it to show the world just how strong you are Beauty.

LOVE -BEAST

I OPEN the box and find a gorgeous necklace with the inscription "You are my Beauty and my Beast." I wipe a tear from my cheek as I smile at the necklace. It's beautiful and it's just what I need today. I can face whatever people say about me. They can call me sick, a criminal. They can say that Nacio should be locked up in jail. I don't care. I'm strong enough to face them.

I put the necklace on over my black dress that I wore today. I feel like a beast in the dress and necklace.

I hear a knock at the door followed by, "Thank god you are back. I need a vacation."

I smile when I hear his voice. I glance up at Preston standing in my doorway his arms crossed across his chest. He's changed since the last time I saw him. He stands taller when he walks into a room. His voice is deeper and more in control of what he wants. He hasn't just survived these last few months without me, he's flourished and turned into an amazing vice president.

I smile. "You can take as long of a vacation as you need. You deserve it."

He steps into my office and closes the door behind him. "Nah. I don't really want a vacation. I just wanted you back. I missed you."

I get up from behind my desk and go over and hug him. "I missed you too."

Preston's phone vibrates and I let go of him and return to my desk. Preston talks for a minute while I pull up my email on my computer. I have thousands and thousands of emails. So many that with every second that passes the number ticks up higher and higher trying to process them all.

My eyes widen. I'm going to have to figure out how to just delete them all and start over. There is no way I will be able to get through all of them even if I spent all of my time going through them for the next year.

Preston ends his call and says, "You only have five minutes to answer your email, then you have a meeting with Madeline, followed by a meeting with—"

"Preston."

"What?"

I cock my head to the side. "You are not my assistant. You are my vice president. You don't need to rattle off my schedule to me anymore, that's way below your pay grade. Just because I'm back doesn't mean you go back to being my assistant. You've done great work since I've been gone and I want you to continue that work, not go back to being my assistant."

"But you need me and I need to go back to being your assistant. I miss you."

I shake my head. "You are not going back to being my assistant."

"But I want to work with you. I don't want to be stuck in an office on a different floor and never see each other."

I frown. I don't want that either. "You'll move your office next door to me then. I want you near me too. You are the best employee I have and one of my best friends. I want to hear your opinion about everything."

He thinks for a moment. "Done."

"Good. Now I just need to find a new assistant to help arrange all of that."

Preston frowns.

"Don't worry, whoever I hire I won't like as much as I like you."

"Good. Now until then I'm going to act as your assistant until you get back up to speed and find someone new."

"No, you are my vice president."

"No, I'm on vacation as your vice president. Today I'm just your assistant."

A knock at my door stops the arguing.

"Come in," I shout.

The door opens and Jake stands in the door. I frown. "I thought I made myself clear you were to find another job."

"You did and I did."

"Then why are you here?" I narrow my eyes at him ready for a fight.

Jake glances from me to Preston who is also giving him a dirty look. He slowly turns his gaze back to me.

"To say I'm sorry. For everything."

My eyes narrow in confusion. I was expecting a lot of things from Jake, but I never expected him to apologize.

He takes a step forward and Preston takes a step closer ready to step in between us if he needs to. Jake doesn't even glance his way.

"I know you're happy. I know you chose a man that is right for you. You obviously wanted danger and excitement, while I'm boring. I just couldn't stop myself because I've been in love with you all these years. I love you and that made me do all sorts of stupid things. Things I deeply regret."

He takes a step forward again.

"It's okay. I understand. I've done some stupid things I regret for love as well."

He shakes his head. "What I did was worse."

A small grin sneaks onto my lips. "I doubt that."

His eyes scan my body. "I just wanted to tell you I'm sorry, but I'm glad you're happy. I won't cause you any more trouble."

"You didn't cause me any trouble. Not really." Not compared to everything else I've been through.

"And I'm sorry for what I'm about to do."

I raise my eyebrows, but before I can realize what he is doing his lips are on mine. It's a short kiss. His lips barely brush mine before they are suddenly gone. Preston pushes Jake back.

"I'm sorry," he says with sad eyes as Preston pushes him out of my office.

I'm not sorry though because it felt like the closure he needed.

Preston returns to my office. "I'll tell security to make sure that Jake never steps foot inside this building again."

I nod, although I don't think it will be necessary. Jake won't bother me anymore. Reina won't either. The FBI won't. We have no enemies left. I can finally be happy. We can finally be happy.

"Come on Preston, we have a meeting to get to."

I walk out of my office no longer afraid of what people are going to say to me. I am the boss after all, if anyone disapproves of our relationship I can fire them. They don't deserve to work for my company anyway if they feel that way about me.

I PLOP BACK into my office chair after an exhausting and thrilling morning. Every person that I met with today was excited to hear about my engagement. They wanted to know all of the details of when we were getting married and what I would be wearing. Nobody cared who Nacio is or what he has done. At least not beyond the superficial level. I worried about our two worlds colliding for nothing. Everyone here is excited to meet him. I'll have to make sure he stops by the office sometime later this week.

I hear a knock on my door and I hope it's Nacio although I know it's not. He has been away the last two nights on FBI business.

"Come in," I shout toward the door.

The door opens and Kinsley comes in carrying a bag of take out and baby Kiera.

I jump out of my chair and run over and take Kiera from Kinsley's arms. She smiles at me as I grab her and spin her around.

"What are you two doing here?"

"We wanted to bring you lunch on your first day back," Kinsley says.

"Perfect timing, I'm starving."

"Good, because I brought lots of yummy Mexican food that I can't eat all by myself."

Kinsley walks over to my desk and begins unpacking our lunch while I carry Kiera over to the couch and sit down with her on my lap.

"You've gotten so big Kiera. I'm going to have to get you some more clothes since your old stuff won't fit much longer."

"You have got to stop spoiling Kiera, Scarlett. Her closet is already completely filled. I'm pretty sure she has more clothes than I do. If you get her any more, I'm going to have to find a second closet for her," Kinsley says.

I look down at my niece, who is grabbing onto the necklace around my neck and trying to put it in her mouth. "I can spoil her as much as I want. I gave birth to her, and I'm her aunt, so I get to spoil her."

Kinsley laughs. "Fine, I guess you do."

I kiss Kiera on the cheek for about the millionth time since she got here.

Kinsley pulls out some chips and salsa and brings it over. I dig in immediately as Kiera continues playing with my necklace while sitting in my lap.

"Are you still planning on having dinner with us tonight?"

I sigh. "Yes, I'm just not sure if Nacio will make it or not. He's working on a case for the FBI and I don't think he will be done and home in time for dinner tonight."

"I could tell Killian that it could just be a girls night tonight, just the three of us."

I shake my head. "That's okay. If Killian is there to distract you then it means I get more time with this cutie." I kiss Kiera's cheek again. "I just can't get enough of her."

"I know. It's why she loves you so much."

Kiera looks at her mom holding her arms out. She may love me, but she still knows who her mom is. She cries when I don't immediately turn her over to Kinsley.

"She's hungry," Kinsley says pulling out a bottle, I take it and then Kiera is happy to stay in my lap as long as I feed her.

"I'm just glad I don't have to deal with the three a.m. feedings like you do. I'm not sure I'm ready for that yet."

Kinsley smiles. "Well, she rarely wakes up in the middle of the night anymore. The first few months we brought her home were hard, but whenever you and Nacio decide it's time to have one of your own, you'll find a way to be ready."

"You think he will make a good dad?"

She smiles. "I think he will make a great dad."

I nod and think back to Kiera's birth. If he is anything like he was that day, he will make a great dad.

I LIE in bed pretending to sleep so that Nacio will sleep. I don't think he has slept at all this week so far. Instead, he has been by my side worrying about all the possibilities that could go wrong when I deliver this baby.

I've been too uncomfortable to sleep much this week so he hasn't slept either. So instead of spending my night reading or watching TV or asking him to rub my back or feet I'm pretending to sleep so that he can sleep. But from the tightening pain in my stomach that is growing more intense by the second I don't think he's going to get much sleep tonight either.

Another contraction hits me and I know despite being one in the morning that I can't wait. I need to get to the hospital.

"Nacio," I whisper when the contraction is over.

He moans.

194

"Nacio," I say a little lighter as I push on his shoulder to get him to wake up.

He does, popping out of bed.

"Are you okay? Is it time?"

I nod. "It's time."

His eyes pop as panic fills his eyes. For just a second he stands frozen trying to figure out what to do and then the second passes and he moves into action.

He runs to the closet and grabs our bag for the hospital and somewhere along the way back to me he threw on some jeans and a shirt of his own. He slings the bag over his shoulder and then is on my side of the bed helping me stand up.

He starts guiding me out of the bedroom when I stop. "I need to change first."

He looks at me like I'm crazy. "I'm not wearing my pajamas to the hospital."

He frowns. "Yes you are. We need to get you to the hospital now and as soon as you get there they are going to have you change into a hospital gown anyway."

"But I look—"

He kisses me to shut me up. It works because I no longer care what I'm wearing when we stop kissing. Nacio begins leading me out of our apartment and into his Mercedes and then we are speeding toward the hospital as I have another contraction. He holds out his hand for me through the whole contraction as he says in the calmest voice I have ever heard, "Breathe. Imagine the pain leaving your body."

His words are exactly what I need.

THE WHOLE HOSPITAL stay he is exactly what I need. Through all twenty-two hours of labor. He held my hand. Said the right words. Got me ice chips. Made sure Kinsley and Killian were there and taken care of. He did everything perfectly until Kiera was born. Until the emergency, that I can remember more than the pain of giving birth.

"*She's hemorrhaging,*" *the doctor says.*

"*What?*" *I ask, but I never hear the doctor's response. I know she gives one because Nacio listens intently but the pain is too much for me to focus on silly things like words.*

I scream while Nacio grabs hold of my hand. He says words, but again I don't hear them.

I begin to feel light headed after the immediate pain and hope that maybe I'll pass out so I don't have to deal with the pain, but Nacio grabs my face focusing my eyes on his and I know I'm not supposed to close my eyes. So I keep them open and deal with the pain with him. His eyes calm me even though I can see his mouth moving and I know he is probably saying something comforting, it's his eyes that stay so calm, so loving, that keeps me calm.

I don't know how long it takes to get the bleeding to stop. But it must because the pain slows. I can finally hear words again.

"*The bleeding stopped. You are going to make a full recovery,*" *the doctor says.*

Nacio grabs hold of my head and kisses me hard on the fore-head. When he steps back he finally lets in the fear that he was holding back from me. Intense fear at losing me.

We both cry as we grab onto each other. "*I'm not going anywhere,*" *I whisper into his ear.*

I later learned that the hemorrhaging was bad. Some of the worst the doctor had seen and they were considering whisking me off to surgery to possibly have to have a hysterectomy. I might not have ever been able to have children of my own. I could have died. But despite Nacio knowing that, he stayed by me as my rock. Keeping me calm so that I could survive.

"What's going on with you?" Kinsley asks breaking my thoughts of the memory.

"Nothing."

She studies me. "Something is going on, I just don't know what it is yet."

I smile. "I'm not hiding anything from you. I promised you I wouldn't ever again."

She smiles, but I can tell she's still suspicious.

I turn my attention back to Kiera. I'm not hiding anything. You can't hide the truth when you don't know what the truth is yet.

BEAST

"Reina, I have to go, I'm kind of in the middle of something," I say into the phone that I stupidly answered instead of doing my job.

"Then tell me yes. Tell me that you will let me find you a new apartment for you and Scarlett. You two can't survive living in her apartment forever. It's dull and tiny and not yours. It will always be hers."

I sigh. She's not going to let this go until I give in and tell her yes. Although, I don't need a new apartment. Scarlett's apartment is more than adequate and I really don't care where I live as long as I have her with me; that's all I want anymore.

I hear a moan escape the throat of Clint, the man I tied up to a chair with duct tape. I smile. Scarlett may be all I want anymore, but I still crave the blood. I still need to let the beast out every once in a while and I can't believe Scarlett, or the FBI for that matter, lets me do it.

"I really need to go Reina."

"Then tell me you will let me pick out some apartments for you and Scarlett to look at this weekend? I have some fabulous ones already in mind and with the amount of money you two make you deserve the absolute best."

I laugh. "No, you want to make a killer commission. You don't actually care about where Scarlett and I live."

"I could waive the commission, finding the perfect place for the famous Scarlett Bell and her hot fiancé would help me sell more apartments and homes in the aftermath, but of course I'm not. Just say yes and I'll stop calling you every day."

"Don't you have plenty of clients and money already?"

"Of course, but it's ridiculous that I don't get to help my brother and his future wife find a home."

"That's because we already have a home."

"No, you live in her home."

I run my hand through my hair. There is no arguing with her. And I shouldn't argue with her anyway. It's been clear these last few months that what Reina enjoys is the control and power that comes with running a company. Any company that makes her money, it didn't have to be running a company that involves killing people. I should just shut my mouth and support her.

"Fine, we will go with you this weekend—"

"Yes!"

"But only if Scarlett says yes too."

"Oh, she will. No woman says no to looking for a new, fancy home."

I roll my eyes even though she can't see me and end the

call. I put my phone in my pocket and turn to Clint whose eyes have grown wide showing the whites around his dark brown eyes. I can feel my excitement growing as his fear grows. *Who would have known that I would love torturing people for information just as much as I would like killing them?* Of course I've tortured people in the past, but nothing like what the FBI has me do for information.

I walk over to my box of tools I brought with me to extract the information that I need, although most of the time the most effective form of torture doesn't involve any tools. Still, using tools can be fun. I look to Santino, who has been standing, watching our prisoner. He is supposed to be helping me, but I don't need his help to get the info that I need.

"Leave me and Clint alone now Santino."

Santino gives me a dirty look. He hates it when I don't let him do the fun part of the job, but I feel the beast growing wild inside of me needing to get out. I promised Scarlett that I won't kill or hurt anyone that the FBI doesn't instruct me to. I'll use my dangerous desires to only fight evil, not become part of it. But it's been a while since the FBI has let the monster inside of me out. So I need to enjoy this, without Santino.

I raise my eyebrows at him and he storms out of the mostly empty warehouse.

I turn my attention back to my toolbox trying to decide where I want to start. I run my hand over the array of tools. Drills, knives, hammers, pliers. I pause over the pliers. I need this to last a while so I can let the beast inside run wild. It will help me control my urges in the future. Pliers are a good way to start. If he's really a life-long criminal, he won't reveal anything to me after a few pulled teeth and fingernails.

I pick up the pliers and then turn my attention toward Clint. I walk toward him as I slowly roll up my sleeves.

"I'm not going to lie to you Clint. I need this. I need this to last for hours so that I can control the beast inside me afterwards."

I stop in front of Clint and bend down so that I can look Clint in the eyes. "Can you do that Clint? Can you hold out answering my questions for hours? Or are you going to give in right away?"

Clint groans.

I smile. "Good."

I rip the duct tape off his mouth before I stand up.

Clint screams as soon as the tape is off.

"No one can hear you Clint."

He still screams. They always scream. It doesn't matter how strong the man or woman, when they look death in the face, they scream. They just don't know that I can't kill them. The FBI won't let me. Although, I'm hoping at some point I'll get someone that they want dead and not just information from.

I grab Clint's jaw to keep him from screaming. I crack my neck back and forth. "You're supposed to scream after Clint, not before."

I hold firmly onto his jaw keeping his mouth wide open and I push the pliers inside of his mouth. He struggles trying to close his mouth, but I keep his mouth firmly open as I reach to the molars at the back of his mouth and grab hold of the tooth with my pliers.

His scream gets louder as I make contact with the tooth and begin to pull slowly on the tooth and then suddenly yank it out in one swoop.

Clint screams in agony and struggles against the duct tape holding him to the chair.

I take a deep breath, as the adrenaline takes over my body. I love the feeling.

I punch Clint in the head hard to get him to stop screaming. He does, the shock of the punch to the side of the head enough to get him to stop long enough for me to ask him the question I'm supposed to ask.

"Who do you work for?" I ask even though it's a stupid question. I already know who he works for. He works for a drug organization that operates mostly in Japan and China. So I don't know what the FBI thinks they are going to get from this question. They can at least ask questions that will get better intel.

He blinks a couple of times and then spits blood in my face.

I smile. "Feisty. I knew you would last long enough to soothe the beast inside when I saw you. Let's try pulling another though just to be sure you are up for several hours of torture."

I grab his jaw again as he tries to pull away. He can't get away. He's mine for at least the next three hours. That's my prediction for how long he lasts before he spills his guts. It will be long enough.

I reach the pliers into his mouth, this time going for the molar on his right side instead of his left. I yank this one in one motion not giving him time to get used to the idea.

He screams again.

I close my eyes loving the sound. I crack my neck again as I think of all the things I can do next. The damage I can do.

My eyes fly open when the screaming stops. It's too early for him to stop screaming. Clint is lunched over in his chair. His head flops against his chest.

I sigh. So much for lasting hours of torture. Two teeth

pulled and he already passed out from the pain. I grab his head and lift it up hoping he's still conscious enough that if I smack him in the face he will wake so that we can continue. When I lift his head though it plops back and it doesn't look like he's breathing. I place two fingers against his neck checking for a heartbeat that I can't find.

Dammit. "Santino!" I yell toward the door of the warehouse that he disappeared behind.

I run to the toolkit and pull out a knife and then begin ripping off the tape weary that he could be faking it to get me to remove the duct tape, but I've never seen anyone good enough to fake no pulse.

"What did you do?" Santino asks from behind me.

"Just help me."

Santino begins helping me untie Clint. When all the bindings are off we pull him to the floor and begin CPR. After a couple minutes pass, we both realize our efforts are futile.

"You killed another one? This is the second one in—"

"Three months."

"They are going to fire you. Or throw you in jail. You weren't supposed to kill him."

I roll my eyes. "I know I wasn't. It wasn't like I meant to either of the times. I yanked two teeth. How was I supposed to know that pulling two teeth would cause a heart attack or whatever this guy suffered from?"

Santino narrows his eyes at me trying to decide if all I did was pull a couple of teeth. "And what was your excuse last time?"

"The drill slipped."

"Please tell me he at least told you who he works for before he croaked."

I shrug. "We already know who he worked for."

"They are going to fire you."

I sigh. He's probably right. They weren't too happy the last time this happened. They didn't give me any jobs for three months. That's too long to go without hurting someone.

I pull out my phone.

"What are you doing?" Santino asks.

"I'm going to call Killian. He still has some pull with the FBI, maybe he can help."

I dial his number and wait for him to answer.

"What happened?" Killian answers.

I frown. "Nothing happened. Can't I call one of my closest friends for a chat?"

"No."

I exhale deeply. "Okay fine. I accidentally killed the guy I was just supposed to torture for information."

"Goddammit Nacio. Can't you at least try to keep them alive."

"I did. Honestly, I just pulled two teeth."

"I'm sure that's all that happened."

"Can you fix this?"

"Yea, but this is the last time Nacio. Next time you are on your own."

I smile.

"Are you going to make it to dinner tonight? Kinsley and I are having everyone over for dinner."

"Yea, I should make it back. It won't take long to clean up. It never takes long to clean up a dead body."

I can feel Killian frowning on the other end of the line.

"I didn't do it on purpose."

Killian doesn't answer. He just ends the call and I begin helping Santino clean up the body.

"You going over to Kinsley and Killian's tonight for dinner?"

"Yep and I'm bringing a date."

I raise my eyebrows. Dinner just got a lot more interesting.

***

SCARLETT

I GET BACK to my apartment that Nacio now shares with me. I hear the shower running upstairs which makes me smile. I didn't think he would make it home tonight but I'm glad he's home and can go to dinner with me tonight. I've missed him these last couple of nights, but I know he needed this. I could see with every day that passed the beast inside him struggled to get out and he struggled to keep him buried inside.

Now I can tell him that Reina called wanting us to go look at apartments with her this weekend. And that I said yes. It's been something I have been wanting to do for a while now. Go apartment shopping, but I wanted to wait to tell him my other news first. Now is the perfect time for both.

I start heading upstairs to bathroom and in perfect timing Nacio steps out of the bathroom with a towel wrapped around his waist.

I stop walking to admire him with what I'm sure is a goofy smile on my face. "Glad you're home. I missed you." I walk over and kiss him on the lips.

When I pull away, I see the cut on his lip and the bruise just below his eye. It should bother me seeing the danger that he was in. The evidence that he just did something bad to someone else. It doesn't bother me though. It makes me happy to see him doing what makes him happy even if I don't fully understand it. At least now he is working for good instead of evil.

I know that is who he is, and I'm not going to try to change him. I have just learned not to ask when he comes home looking like he does now. I don't want to worry that he might die or get sent back to prison every time he leaves the apartment.

"We need to get dressed, so we can leave for Kinsley and Killian's dinner in twenty minutes."

Nacio smiles and then flips off the lights in the apartment. "How about I do naughty things to you first?"

I giggle as he kisses my neck. "We can't. We will be late," I whine as Nacio pulls my arms together and then above my head, like he did the first time we met. And I know that's what he wants to do—relive the excitement of that night. "We don't have time for that tonight. Haven't you had enough excitement for one day?"

"Yes," he breathes seriously into my ear. "I have. I'm tired of the same old excitement that used to control my life. I'm ready for a new kind of excitement."

His lips kiss my neck, and I moan.

"Yeah, and what's that?"

"The excitement that comes with getting married and starting a family."

I freeze. That sounds perfect to me, but I don't think he understands that it might not be as exciting as he thinks it will be. "That's normal though. We don't do normal."

"We do when it's an exciting adventure that we are both ready for."

I laugh. "Let's start with getting married first, and then we can do the whole baby thing."

"Fine. But that doesn't mean we can't enjoy the fun and excitement of trying."

I giggle again as Nacio tugs my arms high over my head. We are going to be late to our dinner, but I don't care. I get to fuck my fiancé in the dark while imagining our lives being filled with babies and boring but exciting things, like feedings at three a.m.

It sounds like the perfect way to start our forever.

"We are just going to have to move the wedding up quite a bit because...I'm pregnant."

BEAST

I'M GOING to be a father, keeps repeating in my head. I'm going to be a husband and fast, like tomorrow if I have my way, although I know Scarlett is going to want a big beautiful expensive wedding, not a quick court wedding. But I will give her everything she wants as long as she marries me now.

Killian opens the door to their apartment with a frown on his face. "You're late."

Scarlett blushes. "We are not that late. Only a half hour. That's not late."

Killian continues to frown.

"Lighten up Kill," Scarlett says walking inside. I follow her.

"I would if Nacio would stick to his job instead of taking things too far," Killian says.

Scarlett turns to look at me. "You killed one again?"

"Don't look at me like that."

"Like what?"

"Like you are disappointed in me. This one was not my fault. I barely did anything to him. He just didn't have the heart to hold up to torture."

Scarlett laughs. "Sure it wasn't your fault. Just like the drill wasn't your fault. It just slipped."

I frown. I should have never told her that story. I should have known I'd live to regret it.

I grab Scarlett's hand and guide her into the dining room that is already full of people. Scarlett lets go of my hand to greet Kinsley who immediately hands her a glass of wine. Scarlett takes it, but she's flustered. She doesn't want to tell people we are pregnant yet. She says it's too early and she wants to plan a quick wedding first, but I don't know how she is going to keep it a secret. I can already see Kinsley eyeing Scarlett suspiciously. I think she gives Scarlett alcohol every time just to test to see if she is pregnant. Scarlett looks across the room to me asking for my help. I just shrug. I find Reina and give her a quick hug before I take a seat next to Santino. Scarlett quickly makes her way back to a spot next to me as she tries to avoid Kinsley although from the smile on Kinsley's lips she has already guessed.

Kinsey knows she won't get any answers from Scarlett so instead she looks to me raising her eyebrows. I wink at her in response. Kinsley claps her hands together excitedly as everyone at the table turns their attention to her.

"I'm sorry. I'm just so excited to finally have everyone together. It's been too long," Kinsley says taking a seat as Killian brings out the last of the food to set on the table.

I lean over to Santino who is sitting next to an empty chair.

"So who is your date?"

He sighs. "She couldn't make it. Had a family emergency."

ELLA MILES

I roll my eyes. "Sure she did." I don't believe for a second that he actually has a girlfriend. It's been years since I've seen him with anyone serious.

Kinsley grabs her glass of wine and lifts it. "I want to propose a toast..."

Scarlett shoots daggers with her eyes at me thinking I told Kinsley about our pregnancy. I smile at her not caring who knows or what the rules are about when you are supposed to tell people. I hope Kinsley is announcing it to everyone although I doubt that she is.

"I'm so thankful to have every one of you in my life. New and old friends. We consider you all family now and no matter what happened in the past between us, I know that now we are all one family. To family." She raises her glass.

"To family," everyone says as we clink our wine glasses before all taking a sip. I watch as Scarlett awkwardly takes a sip as well, obviously worried about how she's not going to drink tonight.

I glance to Santino to my left. He's my brother. He's always been family but even still we haven't always had the perfect relationship but we know we will be there for each other no matter what. And if he is really dating someone we will all be happy to invite her into our world as soon as he's ready.

I glance past the empty chair next to Santino to Reina. She looks happy. Happier than I've ever seen her as she chats with Preston on her left. Who also looks happy although I don't know him well enough to know when he's not happy.

I glance to Kinsley and Killian. Both sitting at a table where at least three people have tried to kill one or both of them. They have been so forgiving. So welcoming over these last few months and I couldn't imagine ever killing them now.

I reach down and take Scarlett's hand in my lap that is shaking slightly as I whisper into her ear, "Don't worry about the wine. I'll drink it for you. No one will know."

She smiles.

I glance around the room. I would kill for anyone in this room and I can't think of living without any one of them. I have a family now. A real family that cares more about loving one another than killing. I glance down at Scarlett's stomach, and I have a growing family that is just going to get larger and larger if I have it my way.

I have a family. A family that forgives me when I mess up. A family that doesn't expect anything from me. A family that loves me. A family that is mine, forever.

The End

Thank you so much for reading!

Grab your FREE copy of Not Sorry
here→EllaMiles.com/freebooks

FREE BOOKS

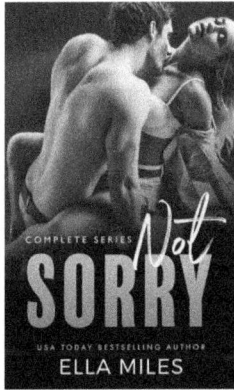

Read **Not Sorry** for **FREE**! And sign up to get my latest releases, updates, and more goodies here→EllaMiles.com/freebooks

Follow me on BookBub to get notified of my new releases and recommendations here→Follow on BookBub Here

Free Books

Join Ella's Bellas FB group for giveaways and FUN→Join
Ella's Bellas Here

Dirty Addiction

Dirty Revenge

ALIGNED SERIES:

Aligned: Volume 1 (Free Series Starter)

Aligned: Volume 2

Aligned: Volume 3

Aligned: Volume 4

Aligned: The Complete Series Boxset

UNFORGIVABLE SERIES:

Heart of a Thief

Heart of a Liar

Heart of a Prick

Unforgivable: The Complete Series Boxset

STANDALONES:

Pretend I'm Yours

Finding Perfect

Savage Love

Too Much

Not Sorry

ABOUT THE AUTHOR

Ella Miles writes steamy romance, including everything from dark suspense romance that will leave you on the edge of your seat to contemporary romance that will leave you laughing out loud or crying. Most importantly, she wants you to feel everything her characters feel as you read.

Ella is currently living her own happily ever after near the Rocky Mountains with her high school sweetheart husband. Her heart is also taken by her goofy five year old black lab who is scared of everything, including her own shadow.

Ella is a USA Today Bestselling Author & Top 50 Bestselling Author.

Stalk Ella at:
www.ellamiles.com
ella@ellamiles.com